WHO KILLED HILDA MURRELL?

By Judith Cook

Directors Theatre: Harrap, 1974
National Theatre: Harrap, 1976
Apprentices of Freedom: Quartet, 1979
Women in Shakespeare: Harrap, 1982
Portrait of a Poison – 245T (with Chris Kaufman): Pluto, 1982
Shakespeare's Players: Harrap, 1983
Close to the Earth: Routledge & Kegan Paul, 1984
The Waste Remains and Kills: Pluto, 1984 (fiction)
As I Walked Out to Lyonesse: Hodge, 1984
The Price of Freedom: New English Library, 1985

WHO KILLED HILDA MURRELL?

Judith Cook

NEW ENGLISH LIBRARY

A New English Library Original Publication, 1985

First NEL Paperback Edition June 1985

NEL Books are published by
New English Library
Mill Road, Dunton Green,
Sevenoaks, Kent.
Editorial office: 47 Bedford Square, London WC1B 3DP

Typeset by Rowland Phototypesetting Ltd
Bury St Edmunds, Suffolk

Printed in Great Britain by
Richard Clay (The Chaucer Press) Ltd
Bungay, Suffolk

British Library C.I.P.

Cook, Judith
    Who killed Hilda Murrell?
    1. Murrell, Hilda   2. Murder—England
    I. Title
    364.1'523'0924   HV6535.G7

ISBN 0-450-05885-9

CONTENTS

Acknowledgments

I WOULD like, first of all, to thank Hugh Stephenson and the staff of the *New Statesman* for backing me on the Hilda Murrell story for I feel that without them the story might well not have appeared at all.

A fast book like this requires a great deal of assistance and co-operation from many people and I must thank Colin Honnor for being such a supportive editor, and his assistant, Alice Atkin. I acknowledge with gratitude the assistance and help I received from Tam Dalyell MP, Robin Corbett MP, John Halkes, ex chairman of Friends of the Earth, and all those who helped by supplying material for this book. I would like to thank Commander Green for permission to reprint his aunt's paper on nuclear waste which was read at the Sizewell enquiry in September 1984. Finally, a special thank you to Angela Baker who typed out the manuscript from my own very annotated typescript and made it comprehensible.

Author's Note

THE POLICIES of the State are the policies of the government in power – that was the summing up by Mr Justice McCowan at the end of the trial of the senior civil servant, Clive Ponting, tried under section 2 of the 1911 Official Secrets Act for leaking documents connected with the sinking of the Argentine cruiser, *General Belgrano*, to Labour MP Tam Dalyell. The jury disagreed and acquitted Mr Ponting.

But this chilling statement made by a High Court judge typifies the climate of the times in Britain in 1985, a country so proud of its democratic freedoms, its right to protest and to criticise. Never can we have heard so much prating from politicians about how fortunate we are to have so much freedom and how our democratic system is the best in the world and how fortunate we are compared with almost anywhere else. Yet, increasingly over recent years, our civil liberties have been under constant threat and erosion in the name of that very freedom and democracy and those who disagree with the policies of the government in power are seen, in Mrs Thatcher's own words as 'the enemy within'.

Hilda Murrell was murdered on March 21st, 1984. I first noticed it when I read the *Guardian* on August 18th, 1984 where I saw that a distinguished seventy-eight-year-old rose grower had been murdered before she was able to present the paper on nuclear waste on which she was working, to the Sizewell enquiry. There was also a précis of that paper. It did sound rather odd but I put it out of my mind and got on with the task in hand, writing a book on a very different subject indeed.

At the end of August 1984 I had a telephone call from a member of staff at Pluto Press, the publisher who had published a book on the herbicide 245T of which I was co-author, and also of a thriller I had written based on a most bizarre story of an accident at the government's chemical warfare research plant at Nancekuke in Cornwall in the 1960s. One of those who had read the book was a friend of Hilda Murrell and she had rung another friend, at Pluto Press, expressing fears that there had also been a cover up of the events surrounding the death of Hilda Murrell. It was suggested I might look into it.

With extreme reluctance and without the backing of a newspaper which would have made it all much easier and far less fraught, I began to investigate the circumstances surrounding the death of Hilda Murrell. The more I enquired, and most particularly after meeting her nephew, Commander Robert Green and his wife, Liz, the more I became convinced that there was something about the murder which was very wrong indeed – something beyond the horror that murder always brings in its train. It seemed that the 'facts' as told by the police to local papers and to Miss Murrell's family, just did not add up with what actually appeared to have happened. Wherever you looked, you found a most extraordinary story.

There were three reasons for keeping on with the story. The first was an instinct that something was badly wrong and needed to be aired. The second was anger that two most decent people, like Rob and Liz Green, had found themselves caught up in a really nightmarish situation through no fault of their own, and the third is purely personal. I became interested in the character of Hilda Murrell herself, a most redoubtable woman of a type which has virtually disappeared. My own mother-in-law, Nan

Green, was just such another independent minded protestor. She had gone to Spain and worked with the Fifth International Brigade during the Spanish Civil War (her husband died in the fighting); she was a great fighter against what she saw as injustice and up until her death two weeks after that of Hilda Murrell and at the same age (though from natural causes) she had been involved with the Greenham Common women. Had she lived she would have been encouraging me enthusiastically in my investigation into the death of such a sympathetic contemporary. What, I thought, would we have felt had she too been found dead in such suspicious circumstances?

I first attempted to get the results of my investigation published in the *Guardian*. Having failed dismally, I turned to Hugh Stephenson and the *New Statesman* and it is entirely thanks to him that the story broke at all.

There was a lull for a short while after its publication on November 9th, 1984 and it was during this time that I was contacted by MP Tam Dalyell. Some weeks later, the night before he launched his offensive on Hilda Murrell's death in the House of Commons on the night of December 19/20th, 1984, he rang me to tell me what he intended to say. Many of the facts were new to me.

Following his intervention a constant stream of information has trickled in to all of us who have followed the case. We have all, as it were, found various pieces of a jigsaw puzzle which fit together although none of them as yet complete the picture.

I advance no personal theories as to manner of Hilda Murrell's death. I must admit that unlike Tam Dalyell I do not have a touching faith in the way the nuclear industry conducts itself, especially when there is as much at stake as at present and I think Hilda Murrell's anti nuclear activities could have been a possible motive for a break-in to her house or they could have provided a joint motive with what was to become known as 'the *Belgrano* connection'.

If Hilda Murrell did not meet her death at the hands of an ordinary passing burglar then who did kill her? We will look at the various security services who might have been involved in the controversy surrounding such a break-in. I am now personally convinced that whoever it was she surprised in her house that Wednesday morning in March 1984, it was not just a simple thief who happened to have chosen that precise time to do a spot of breaking and entering.

Strange events surrounded Hilda Murrell's death and they continue. Odd things happen, too, to those who have looked into it. Since we have no way of discovering, in this democratic country of ours, if our telephones are being tapped in an unauthorised fashion, most investigative journalists assume they are and act accordingly. But when all your letters arrive not only late but obviously having been tampered with, then you do become just a little suspicious.

The American newspapers and television have called Hilda Murrell's death the 'British Karen Silkwood case . . .' seeing a parallel between Hilda's murder and the death of the young woman, in most suspicious circumstances, just before she blew the gaffe on the lack of safety standards at the plutonium plant at which she worked. But Hilda Murrell's story is even more complicated than that for, quite innocently, she could have been inextricably bound up in the whole business of the mystery surrounding the decision to sink the *Belgrano* and the subsequent misleading statements in Parliament.

Colin Honnor of New English Library first seized on the idea of the Hilda Murrell murder as being a subject for a book before I had managed to get the first piece on the subject published and while he and I were working on the publication of my book on official secrecy, *The Price of Freedom*, which NEL were to publish early in 1985. At that stage I did not see how it could make a book. Subsequently, although I had wanted to put the story of her death behind me, I felt haunted by her and changed my mind.

The statement made by Mr Justice McCowan is not just worrying in the context of the Ponting trial, it has even more terrifying implications for at the end of that particular road lie the Gulag Archipelago and the gas ovens of Dachau. Those who opposed Hitler could have been said to be opposing the State in general, not the Fascist policies of his government in particular. Asking the jury to acquit Clive Ponting, his defence counsel said: 'If what he did was a crime, God help us – for no government will.'

It is against this background that we look into the strange death of Hilda Murrell.

Judith Cook
Newlyn, Cornwall, 1985

ONE

Death of a Rose Grower

ON THE morning of Saturday March 24th, 1984 the body of an elderly woman was found in a copse just outside Shrewsbury. She had been murdered. Her name was Hilda Murrell, a seventy-eight-year-old rose grower and one of the world's leading authorities on the subject. She had been born and bred in Shrewsbury, was educated at the local high school and then went on to Newnham College, Cambridge, where she read English, modern and medieval languages, and French. She took her finals but, as was the position at that time, was unable until later to collect her degree. Eminent women such as Dorothy L. Sayers, D. K. Broster and Vera Brittain had found themselves similarly placed at Oxford.

After coming down from university she joined her grandfather's firm and set about becoming a specialist in the growing of roses, in particular very old species and miniatures. She took gold awards at all the major flower shows including Chelsea.

She is described by family and friends as having been a very strong-minded woman and for many years she ran the rose-growing business by herself. She was also, according to her nephew, Robert Green, 'a very private person'. She had fought a disability all her life – she was born blind in one eye – and at the time of her death was suffering from arthritis, but was still strong and healthy for her age. She liked walking and drove her own car.

During the war she worked with the Jewish Refugee Children's Society, placing the children who had escaped from Hitler's Europe into suitable homes. She was a Liberal Party supporter and a member of Tories Against Cruise and Trident (TACT), and she had sent donations to the women's peace camp at Greenham Common near Newbury.

In 1962 she became one of the founder members of the Shropshire Trust for Nature Conservation as she had a deep concern for conservation and the environment.

Her love of plants and growing things did not end with her work. At her bungalow in Wales at Llanymynech, which she called her 'shack', she had a marvellous garden full of unusual and rare plants. In Wales, too, she continued with her conservation interests, becoming a member of the management committee of the Llanymynech Rocks Nature Reserve. She was a pillar of respectability.

So how did this woman – described by Percy Thrower, who, in 1970, had bought her rose nursery from her, as 'one of the world's greatest authorities on old-fashioned and shrub roses' – come to be found dead in a copse?

We will begin with the police view of the case taken from their own press briefings and reports issued by them to the local papers, in particular the *Shropshire Star*. The area is under the control of the West Mercia Police Authority and the local divisional police headquarters is in Shrewsbury.

The story broke in the *Shropshire Star* on Monday March 26th. The headline was 'Rose Expert Is Murdered'. There was a picture of Hilda wearing one of the floppy hats she favoured (she felt it helped conceal her blind eye), another of the number of her car and pictures of police at work. The report which the police gave to the paper states specifically that she had been found brutally murdered 'and her home in Shrewsbury ransacked'. That needs to be noted carefully.

The report said she had suffered 'multiple stab wounds',

and that the body appeared to have lain where it was found for 'several days'. Robbery was a possible motive for murder. Leading the enquiry was Detective Chief Superintendent David Cole of West Mercia CID. He had been the number two on what became known as the Black Panther case, and the investigation into the death of young Lesley Whittle, and it was he who led the enquiry into the Geoffrey Prime spy scandal at General Communications Headquarters (GCHQ), Cheltenham, in 1983.

Cole told the press that the last time Hilda Murrell had been seen was when shopping in Shrewsbury on the Wednesday morning (March 21st) at 11 a.m. and her car had been seen, near where her body was eventually found, at about 1 p.m. the same morning. He also said that the car had been reported to the police but had been treated as an abandoned vehicle. 'On Friday evening it was still there and police then visited her house, obtained no reply and returned on Saturday.' They then 'forced entry'.

Her home, a detached Victorian house near the outskirts of Shrewsbury in Sutton Road, was some six miles from where she was found. She lived alone. Haughmond Hill, near where her body was found, is in a conservation area, popular with walkers, and it may have been thought that she was going there for a walk, although her body was discovered on private land at Hunkington in a small copse.

The next day the headlines in the *Shropshire Star* ran 'Knife Find At Murder Scene'. A bread-knife and Hilda's floppy hat had been discovered near the place where she had been 'left to die'. Detective Chief Superintendent Barrie Mayne, Cole's deputy, said police 'were now working on the theory that Miss Murrell may have returned to her home in Sutton Road . . . to find a robbery in progress'. He gave her age as seventy-four. He confirmed her car had been found slewed in a ditch some 800 yards away from the body. It was not clear whether she had been stabbed at her home, in the car, or at the scene.

The theory was then put forward, which has been promi-

nent ever since in police thinking, that Miss Murrell's
'attacker may have been a local man' although it was
'rather odd' that she had been taken to that particular
area.

Keeping the story going, the headline on Wednesday
March 28th was 'Police Fear Cover Up', a phrase which
came to imply something quite different in the later stages
of the investigation into Hilda Murrell's death. Someone,
said the police, could be shielding her murderer who might
have had bloodstained clothing. That someone could be
'withholding information'. The police statement also said
that police believed the killer may have driven the victim
past the divisional police headquarters in Shrewsbury on
the way to the lonely wood at Hunkington near Haughmond Hill 'where she was left dying'. The police also
released the information that there had been a sighting of
the car being driven along Telford Way, close to the
Severn Acres Club by a 'male person'. Further details were
released of the person who was to become known as 'the
running man'. He was described as aged about thirty, five
feet six inches tall, slim and with fair hair. He wore a
grey jacket and trousers which may have been a suit and
thick-soled trainer shoes. He was seen leaving Hunkington
at lunch-time on the fatal Wednesday, heading towards
Haughmond Hill and later, at 2.30 p.m., in Sundorne Road
nearby.

If you had read the headline over the police press releases for Thursday March 29th, you might have been
forgiven for thinking the murderer was as good as caught.
'Police Net Closing In' cried the *Shropshire Star* in a banner
headline. 'The net is tightening around the brutal killer of
Hilda Murrell. Police say they are close and that they need
just one vital breakthrough. They believe the public holds
the key. That was the dramatic news today from the
man leading sixty police officers in the hunt in one of
Shropshire's most savage murders.' Police also revealed
that Hilda's phone had been 'torn out'. That must be noted

too, for later contradictions appeared as to whether four wires had been disconnected in a professional manner, or whether the line had been yanked out.

Way down the page, when questioned as to motive, Detective Chief Superintendent David Cole, who had given the press conference, said police enquiries had been unable to establish whether anything had actually been stolen from Miss Murrell's home. They believed nothing had actually gone but pointed out that this was difficult to establish as she lived alone and few people would have had access to the upper floor 'where a struggle had taken place in a bedroom'. He said nothing which could really have led to such a confident headline and he again appealed to witnesses to come forward, particularly anyone who had seen the car driven away or the 'running man'.

By the end of the week, the police were saying that Hilda might have been killed for the sake of fifty pounds which seemed to be missing as she had drawn it from her bank on the morning of her death and no trace had been found of it. Nothing else had been stolen. More witnesses had come forward with offers of help.

Also by the end of the week came the first mention of what was to become one of the prime issues of the whole case. A small inner page report in the *Star* of March 30th revealed that before her death Hilda Murrell had been working on a detailed report on the difficulties surrounding the disposal of nuclear waste, which she had been going to read at the enquiry into the building of a pressurised water nuclear reactor (PWR) at Sizewell in Suffolk, then being held at The Maltings, Snape, near Aldeburgh. Friends who gave the information to the press said that Hilda, who had studied some nuclear physics, had been 'highly critical' of the case for the PWR at Sizewell.

During the first week in April, the police continued to look for the 'running man' and an artist's impression was published showing a large-nosed, square-faced individual with thick, longish hair brushed close to his head. A

re-enaction of his run was made by a police officer dressed
as it had been said the running man was on the day of the
murder. Murder squad detectives assured the public that
no effort was being spared in the hunt for the killer.

We will now jump to mid-April. On April 18th the police
released a statement saying that they remained 'confident'
that the murderer would be caught. 'I am confident, given
the continued support of the public, that we can bring this
matter to a successful conclusion', said Cole. 'The enquiry
is in its third week, so it's still in its early stages. It is not
uncommon for murder enquiries to stretch on for more
than three months.' The police, he said, had now reached
the 'stage of evaluation'. The report was headed 'We'll
Catch The Killer – Police Chief.'

On April 18th it was reported that two petty thieves
had appeared before Shrewsbury Magistrates charged with
stealing the tax disc from Hilda Murrell's car on the day
she was murdered. After the thieves heard about the
murder, they panicked and burned the disc which they had
taken from her car after it had been abandoned in the ditch.
Charles Ronald Bevan (21) and Christopher Raymond
Watton (18) from Shrewsbury and Telford respectively,
admitted stealing the disc. Watton also admitted driving
with no Department of Transport test certificate, while
uninsured and without a driving licence. Bevan was given
a twelve-month conditional discharge and Watton had his
case adjourned while magistrates considered a community
service order. Their defence solicitor said the two young
men had been frightened when they discovered why the
car was in that area. There has never been any explanation
as to how the two young men were traced or if they were
ever questioned as to whether they had seen or heard
anything relevant to the crime, since they must have been
at the car very shortly after it was abandoned. In a *World
in Action* programme *Death of an English Rose* 4.3.85,
papers were reported to be scattered over the back seat
when the car was found; but the programme went on to

say that there was some confusion over these.

Routine enquiries went on, police questioning witnesses who had come forward and appealing for more. Then, on April 19th, they came out with a sensational piece of news 'Sex Attack On Murdered Woman – Police'. The police stated that not only had Hilda Murrell been murdered she had also been the victim of 'a sex attack'. 'Forensic tests have established that she was sexually assaulted at her home in Sutton Road, Shrewsbury, before being driven to her death six miles away in a wood near Haughmond Hill.' There was no evidence of actual rape 'but this is a particularly disgusting thing, an assault of this nature on a seventy-eight-year-old respectable woman,' said Cole. The police varied her age throughout their press releases from seventy-four through to seventy-eight to seventy-nine. The sexual motive, said the police, now opened up 'many more avenues of inquiry'. The police were also looking for a red Ford Escort seen on the Friday before her body had been found, driving slowly past the field. It had driven past three times in the space of ninety minutes. They also wanted information about a large dark car seen on the Thursday after Hilda's murder near to the place where her body was found, and from which a man had been seen to get out and walk over to the copse, returning some fifteen to twenty minutes later.

By May 23rd police enquiries did not seem to be getting very far and a hypnotist was brought in to question key witnesses. Cole admitted this was an 'unusual step' but one which proved how the police were making an 'all-out effort' to catch the murderer. 'The witnesses have undergone the process of hypnosis under strictly controlled conditions to elicit information which they were unable to recall through the normal memory processes.' A medically qualified person had been used to carry out the hypnosis. 'It is the first time in my experience I have found it necessary to use hypnotism,' Cole is quoted as saying.

During the next weeks the police continued looking for

red Escorts and talking to witnesses – the hypnosis did not
seem to have helped – and there was little in the way of
further news. At the beginning of July another picture was
issued, another 'artist's impression' of the wanted man.
This showed a thin-faced, long-jawed man with deep set
eyes and wild, black shaggy hair. Although it did not look
in the least like the first artist's impression police still
maintain it shows the same man as in the first picture. The
news was also released that details of the murder were to
be given on the BBC's *Crimewatch* programme to see if
that brought in any new information.

On Saturday August 18th the *Guardian* ran a piece
by its science correspondent, Anthony Tucker, on Hilda
Murrell's paper for Sizewell headed 'Murder Victim's
Sizewell Scorn' in which she accused government ministers of hiding the facts on nuclear waste. Tucker had
obtained a copy of Hilda's evidence from her nephew,
Robert Green, who was to read his aunt's paper on her
behalf at the Sizewell enquiry. Tucker gave an excellent
précis of Hilda's paper and for the first time some rather
odd facts began to emerge. It appeared that a systematic
search of Hilda's home had taken place. Here papers and
books had probably been moved and sifted through and
then replaced in order. The scene-of-crime video showed
drawers and cupboards partially opened but a generally
tidy interior to the breakfast and living rooms.

On Saturday August 25th, Hilda Murrell's funeral finally
took place, five months after her death. Police joined
mourners at the local crematorium. Cole emphasised that
the hunt for the murderer was still going on, blamed
witnesses for not coming forward with information which
would be helpful and said that some 26,000 records, on
computer, were being checked through which was taking
time.

The final startling piece of news from the West Mercia
police was headlined 'FBI Aids Hunt For Killer' in the
Shropshire Star of September 12th. 'The American FBI

has been brought into the Shropshire Hilda Murrell murder investigation to paint a remarkable picture of her killer. It pointed to a local man, who is a loner and a withdrawn individual, whose identity is probably known – but is being kept hidden – by somebody in Shrewsbury.' West Mercia police proudly announced that they were the first force in Britain to ask the FBI's Behavioural Science Research Department for help in a murder investigation. The unit, which deals with criminal personality profiles, had produced a detailed document on the killer which happily confirmed what the local police already thought.

Said Cole: 'It confirms my view that the offender either lives or works within a reasonable walking distance of Miss Murrell's house but certainly very local to the area.' The FBI report indicated they were looking for a white male, in his thirties, who might well be a loner and an 'unsocialised and withdrawn individual'. His motive was primarily burglary. 'He is probably a habitué of local licensed premises and is likely to be an unskilled worker.'

He appealed once again for help from the public.

The question is, is there anyone in Shrewsbury who is hiding the identity of a relative or friend or is there any employer in the town who can search his memory back to March 24th and can remember anyone being absent on the day, or an unexcused absence for a period of two or three hours in the middle of the day? We know from recent house-to-house enquiries that there is still information available but people are waiting for us to knock on the door before coming forward.

I can understand to a certain extent this attitude but people must appreciate it is highly undesirable that a man who can act in this particular way against a frail seventy-nine-year-old woman should really not be free and in a position to repeat any similar types of action.

Somebody knew his identity and was simply not telling the police.

To sum up then, the gist of the first six months of police enquiries seems to be this, as taken from their own conferences and briefings to the local press: it is a tragic story of an elderly rose-growing lady, found murdered in a copse six miles away from her home. From police reports there was nothing in any of her recent actions which might be considered as controversial, no mention was made of her anti nuclear energy activities. Her house had been ransacked but only fifty pounds, the trivial amount of cash mentioned earlier, was taken. She seemed to have surprised the burglar who, after a struggle, bundled her into her own car and drove her to the copse where she was found. She had received some stab wounds, almost certainly caused by the bread-knife found near her body, but they had not been sufficient to kill her. Hilda Murrell had also been sexually assaulted. After he broke into her house, the murderer had wrenched the telephone out of the wall presumably to prevent any possible call for help. No cause of death was given by the police.

After numerous police enquiries and the use of the FBI special computer print-out the police were convinced they were looking for a loner and a local man. Presumably they were also supposed to be looking for a sexual pervert as they had stated she had been sexually assaulted. The murderer may or may not have been the man, of whom two quite different artist's impressions had been published, seen running away from near where her body was found.

But it was not quite like that.

By August 1984 a number of other people, including myself, had begun to take an interest in the death of Hilda Murrell and some immediately perplexing questions arose to which there have never been any satisfactory answers (quite apart from many other discrepancies which will be dealt with later).

1. Hilda Murrell's house had not been ransacked. In fact after making this statement the police much later admitted it had been searched in what appeared to be an orderly manner. Drawers and cupboards had been carefully opened. As Anthony Tucker had correctly reported in the *Guardian* in August, her books and papers seemed to have been moved and probably gone through but left tidily. All her handbags were open on her kitchen table but only the publicised fifty pounds had been stolen. Later, her gardener described shopping bags in the hall, washing, litter, seed packets and handbags and mail on the floor. There was also undisclosed evidence of a struggle.

2. Hilda Murrell had not been sexually assaulted and this extraordinary statement was only withdrawn following persistent questioning by her family. The 'forensic evidence', said to have proved the sexual assault, has never been released. A man's handkerchief, showing faint semen stains – too faint to permit any possibility of successful identification of blood grouping – had been found in the house. Antigens in the blood would fade with age, making identification even more difficult. There was nothing which directly connected it with her murder.

3. Her telephone had not been torn out. It had been dealt with in a very sophisticated manner indeed. An informed source from within British Telecom was to tell me later that the junction box had been unscrewed and only the green wire cut. Then the box was screwed back on again. There were no 'loose wires' as reported by the police. The result was that while the line was obviously dead to anybody trying to ring out on it, any caller ringing in would hear the phone ringing as if all were in order but the occupant of the house was either out or not answering. Later it was proved that a number of people had rung that particular number but had received no reply over the days before Hilda's body was found.

And this is not the only strange thing about the telephone. It was to transpire at a later date that the telephone in her Welsh holiday home, 'the shack', had not only been tampered with but cut off in a similar manner. It was suggested that a storm had caused lightning to strike a capacitator and damage the telephone. But there had been no storms in Wales during the March 1984 period. And the capacitator looked as though it had been 'hit with something hard'.

In fact there was a great deal which was very strange indeed about the murder of Hilda Murrell.

TWO

Fearful for Her Life

To TRY and piece together what did happen, without the benefit of scores of policemen, a computer, hypnosis and the FBI, we need to start further back in time than Hilda Murrell's murder.

Her interest in nuclear energy and its associated risks had become so consuming that she had decided to look into one aspect in particular, that is the disposal of nuclear waste. In the introduction to her Sizewell paper Hilda describes herself as 'an Ordinary Citizen with a typical middle-class, suburban and small-business management background' and how she had read the Department of the Environment's White Paper on nuclear waste (Command No. 8607) and found it 'very unsatisfactory'. A friend had pointed out that it was relevant to the Sizewell B enquiry and this had turned out to be the case.

Hilda was, however, not exactly a typical middle-class ordinary citizen. She had a fine academic mind and a Master of Art's degree. She could more than hold her own in a masculine-dominated competitive business. She set about finding out as much as she could about the nuclear industry and nuclear physics, even going so far as to attend lectures on the subject at the University of Aberystwyth. She had a number of contacts including Sir Kelvin Spencer who had been adviser to the government in the early days of the country's nuclear power programme. He was the chairman of the committee for the study of the economics of nuclear electricity, funded by the Rowntree Trust and sponsored by the *Ecologist* which produced the report *Nuclear Energy: The Real Cost* in 1982. She was also in touch with Mr Gerard Morgan-Grenville of a Wales based organisation called EcoRopa, an ecological research unit which also produces fact sheets on a number of issues from nuclear power to additives in food.

As Hilda's own paper showed, she also read very widely, her sources ranging from government documents and surveys to international papers on the subject of nuclear waste management. The picture presented in the press, in the early days following her murder, of a slightly eccentric, rather vague English lady who grew nice roses is a long way from the truth.

Her friend Joan Tate, whose husband Clive was a founder member, with Hilda, of the local Shropshire Trust for Nature Conservation says, when quoting *The Times*' obituary which implied that she was eccentric:

> She wasn't – anyone who veers from what is a very narrow norm can easily be labelled eccentric, but actually Hilda was an extremely conventional person in her ways and not in any way anything like the implication [of eccentricity] . . . Hilda was very well known indeed, a very independent lady (nothing like that awful photograph except the hat, she always wore them) and also a very private person, careful with her money, a truthful person in the proper sense. I liked her immensely because of her independence of mind and her persistence in matters in which she thought dishonesty and public lies were involved.

Hilda seems to have worked throughout the winter of 1983/84 on her paper and during that time she spoke regularly about its progress to her nephew, Robert Green. She was close to him and his sister, Stella, no doubt in part because she had never married or had children of her own.

Robert Green had recently taken early retirement from the navy and was living with his wife, Liz, in a converted bakery in the village of Leigh near Sherborne in Dorset. He was training to be a thatcher.

It was in the early part of 1984 that some unnamed fear began to haunt Hilda Murrell. She was not a woman to pour out her heart about her feelings and certainly not one to suffer from paranoid fancies.

On March 12th, 1984, Ian Campbell, who lives at Borth in Dyfed (Wales), spoke at a meeting in Llangollen during the European election campaign. After the meeting, he said in a letter he wrote to MP Tam Dalyell: 'We went to a Labour Party member's home. Late that night she told us that Hilda Murrell [who the Campbells knew] was worried about her safety. The next morning one of her friends came to see us and said the same thing. Later we heard on the twelve o'clock news on March 24th that she had been found dead.' We will look later at what further actions Ian Campbell and his wife, Thalia, took but he emphasises again that 'Hilda was worried about her safety some time before her death.'

But it appears Hilda had been worried some weeks before March 12th. On a date which he is pretty certain was February 25th, Hilda Murrell rang her friend, Morgan-Grenville of EcoRopa. His wife confirms this. He was later to make a statement to this effect both to Rob Green and to the police. Morgan-Grenville was taking a bath and told his wife to tell Hilda that he would ring her back when he was out of it and dressed, but Hilda sounded so agitated and worried that, on his wife's insistence, he left the bath, draped in a towel, and dripped along the corridor to the phone.

Her evident anxiety communicated itself to him but she refused to tell him the cause. She spoke to him for some considerable time and before she rang off she said something remarkable and totally out of character. She said: 'If they don't get me first I want the world to know that one

old woman has seen through their lies.' Morgan-Grenville
says in all the time of his acquaintance with her he had
never heard her say anything remotely like that as she was
such a very reserved woman.

A few days before her death, Hilda made a lunch appointment with two friends who lived near her bungalow in
Wales, Drs John and Alicia Symondson. The arrangement
had been made by phone and she expected to arrive at
their house about 12.30 p.m. She therefore expected to be
out for a fair part of the day.

Wednesday March 21st, 1984

It seems that on the morning of her murder Hilda had had
a few routine things to do before setting off for Wales.
Just after 10 a.m. she drove her car, a white Renault 5,
into Shrewsbury town centre and went to the bank where
she drew out the fifty pounds. A friend saw her shopping
in Safeways a little later, and in the car park where she
had parked her car she met an acquaintance, George
Lowe, who was selling a bungalow opposite to her house.
After some chat both got into their respective cars and, as
it happened, Lowe followed Hilda back and saw her turn
into the driveway up to her house just before twelve noon.

She did not go straight into her house. She called at the
house of Mrs Mary O'Connor who lived opposite at 57
Sutton Way to pay for a raffle ticket she had bought from
her. Mrs O'Connor remembered because the raffle ticket
was fifteen pence and Hilda gave her sixteen pence. Earlier
that morning, Mrs O'Connor told me, a young man had
been hanging round on the pavement in front of her house.
He had short, curly, blond hair, was clean-shaven, wore
jeans and smoked a pipe. Finally she had gone out to have
a closer look at him but he crossed the road and jumped
over a fence.

After chatting for a few minutes, Hilda left Mrs

O'Connor and went in to her own house. Nobody else ever saw her alive except for her murderer.

It is impossible to know exactly just what happened after she entered the house. She obviously went upstairs and it seems very likely that the reason she was found partially clothed was because she was changing to go out for her lunch date. She then either disturbed the intruder(s) or heard a noise and tackled him/them – which she might well have done. There is evidence that she resisted the intruders. There was a struggle in the back bedroom and clothes were later found strewn on the floor. Again, she may have been selecting clothes to wear.

The struggle seems to have moved out of the bedroom, for one of the vertical railings in the upstairs banister had been knocked out and was later found inside the bathroom door. It is likely that it was during this struggle that she received the severe blow under her right eye (the eye in which she had been blind since birth) which was clearly visible when her nephew identified her body the following weekend. It was a heavy blow, he says, but he was told that it would not have been sufficient to kill her. Forensic evidence in police hands would show just what caused the blow. Was it in a fall or with a blunt instrument? It is unlikely that Hilda Murrell would have acquiesced when confronted with her attackers.

Just when she received the small stab wounds in her stomach is not at all clear, whether it was in the house – some bedsheets were found rolled up and wet on the kitchen floor – in the car or in the copse. Presumably had she bled very much, then the police would have been able to determine when the stabbing had taken place. The small stab wounds would be consistent with two possible approaches; one, meeting her attacker head on or, two, being approached from behind, the attacker stabbing without the obvious force needed to inflict a fatal wound.

Then comes one of the most remarkable aspects of the whole affair. One would think that any ordinary burglar,

discovered during a robbery, who had then struggled with
an elderly lady, hit her, possibly stabbed her and left her
for dead, would get out of the house as quickly as possible,
leaving her where she fell and hoping nobody would discover the body until he had got away.

But not this one. He bundled her body into her own car
unseen by the neighbours. He then got into the car and
turned out into the street but he did not go in the obvious
direction if he was bent on a quick getaway. That way he
would have had less than a mile to drive before he hit
open country. Instead, he turned towards the centre of
Shrewsbury. He did not, however, drive into the town centre
but turned off to the right, past the divisional police headquarters of the West Mercia police and out along the
Newport Road, in heavy lunch-time traffic. This required
slowing down at roundabouts and at least one set of traffic
lights. He then turned the car off the road into a lane
running through a thickly wooded area which, her nephew
says, would have been 'ideal' for dumping a body, but
continued out on to open prairie-type fields. At this stage
the car slewed into a ditch and grounded with its sump on
a rock.

Either then, or at some future time, Hilda, alive or dead,
was dragged or carried half a mile across a wheatfield to
the poplar copse where she was found. At that time of the
year there was no cover at all, just grass, and only one
access into the copse.

The whole event is quite remarkable. Her car was driven
so fast and erratically that the police found no fewer than
sixty-nine people who remembered seeing it.

A report in the *Shropshire Star* on March 30th quotes
one witness as saying he had had to take evasive action to
avoid being hit by an erratically driven white Renault. He
described the driver as being tallish, of medium build and
with a narrow white face and darkish collar-length hair.
He put the age at around thirty and said the man was
wearing a jacket which might have been grey. He also

described a woman in the front seat who seemed to be slumped or slouched forward and leaning against the passenger door.

Another witness was a motorcyclist who was one of the people who agreed to be put under hypnosis. He says he stopped behind the car at some lights which had been set up because of roadworks. The newspaper report of the sighting gives the time as being just after 1 p.m.

At 1.20 p.m. Hilda's car was seen by a tenant farmer, John Marsh, who farmed the land around the copse at Hunkington and who was on his way home for his lunch. Later he was to tell Rob Green that even at that stage he felt somehow uneasy about it. There was no more to it, he said, but that strange, uneasy feeling which was reinforced when he returned from his lunch and found the car still there. He tried the door and found it to be unlocked so he looked inside but saw nothing in the car of any significance.

He went back to work but the abandoned car continued to nag at the back of his mind and eventually he rang up his local policeman, PC Paul Davies, who lives nearby at Upton Magna, and told him he had found a Renault car slewed in a ditch. He gave the policeman the number of the car, LNT 917W, and it later transpired that PC Davies duly reported the car with its number to the police in Shrewsbury.

It is shortly after this time, after 2 p.m., that there are reported sightings of the 'running man' as previously described.

When it became obvious that Hilda was late for her lunch date her hosts were surprised as she was the kind of meticulous lady who would have rung up and told them she had been delayed. Dr Alicia Symondson therefore rang Hilda and at first, when the phone rang out and there was no reply, assumed that she was on her way over. A further call later in the day also received no reply. Dr Symondson found that difficult to understand.

Thursday March 22nd

Hilda's white Renault remained in the ditch. That afternoon at approximately 3 p.m. a Mr Ian Scott visited the copse. He is the owner of the land farmed by John Marsh and he went into it to examine trees. He was trying to decide if any should be felled and, if so, which, and he says he covered every bit of the copse as he counted trees and established what to do. It was so early in the year there was little undergrowth. He sticks to the story he told the police after Hilda's body was found and to which he has adhered ever since: that there was no body in the copse on that Thursday afternoon and that there could not have been because if there was he would have seen it. He told me: 'I examined the place so thoroughly I would have seen if there'd been a dead rabbit, let alone a person.'

It was on the same day that, according to the *Shropshire Star* of April 18th, police say a tractor-driver working in a nearby field saw a large dark car drive up the lane. It parked in the gateway to a field and a man was seen to leave it and walk over to the copse where he remained for about twenty minutes before returning to his car and driving away. Car and driver have never been traced.

Friday March 23rd

Various people had tried to contact Hilda during the preceding two days but hearing the telephone ring out assumed she was away, possibly at her bungalow in Wales. It is not known if anybody tried to ring her Welsh home as well but if they did, as the telephone had apparently been cut off in a similar way to that in her Shrewsbury house, it would just have sounded as if the house was untenanted but the telephone in working order. Presumably anyone who tried both just assumed she had gone elsewhere.

At nine in the morning, a neighbour passed Hilda's house and saw that her kitchen door was open. His name is Brian George and he lives nearby and helped Hilda with her garden. He was later to tell the police that he did not bother to investigate as there did not appear to be anything wrong. He was not due to do any more gardening until the following day and the open door merely seemed to show that Hilda was getting on with her housework and had left the door ajar.

At ten thirty that morning, John Marsh went to see if the white Renault was still in the ditch and found it was. He again rang PC Davies who confirmed he had reported the car to the Shrewsbury police. The police were later to give the explanation that the abandoned Renault was treated as one of many abandoned cars in the area. It is likely that investigation of these would take up police manpower and resources.

It was during Friday afternoon that police say a red Escort was seen driving slowly past the field in which the copse stood. It was said to have driven past three times during the space of an hour and a half. The police were later to report that a red Escort had also been seen in Hilda's road at about ten thirty on the previous Wednesday morning.

On Friday evening the police finally followed up the abandoned car but could find nothing sinister about it. However, as they now knew to whom it belonged, a policeman was sent round to Hilda's house who says he found nothing wrong, did not receive an answer to his knock and went away again. Was the back door open then, as it was later found to be?

The last two events of the day, as described by other people, diverge considerably from what the police report as having happened.

Firstly, at about six thirty in the evening, two senior policemen from Shrewsbury police headquarters visited a man who lives in the area. He has a full-time job in

education but is also a professional counsellor to people
with sexual problems, often of a severe nature, and he says
he has excellent relations with the police. Because of the
extremely sensitive nature of his job he wishes to remain
anonymous but he spoke both to Tam Dalyell and myself
in the House of Commons on Tuesday January 15th,
1985. Some time previously he had had an unfortunate
experience with one of the people he had been counselling
who had been violent. On Friday evening the police asked
him if he was 'all right'. He was very surprised and replied
that of course he was. The police then asked him if he
could think of somebody who might have a sexual hang-up
about elderly ladies. Could he think of a loner, a man with
sexual problems, who would be turned on by going into
a woman's bedroom and interfering with her clothing?
Someone who might be violent? After some discussion the
police went away leaving this witness wondering what it
had all been about.

He says: 'I realised when I read the first reports in the
paper the next evening of the finding of Hilda Murrell's
body that it seemed as if the police had been describing
the murder but I'm at a loss to understand why they came
to me on the Friday night when she wasn't supposed to
have been found until the Saturday.'

Saturday March 24th

At 6.30 a.m., the police confirm, they visited Hilda's house
again, first on the scene being the constable who had called
in the night before and received no reply. The constable
said he went inside – later the police were to say they
'forced entry' which does not fit in with Brian George's
statement that her door was open the previous day – and
had a look around, although he didn't go into Hilda's
bedroom as he thought she might be in it. Her kitchen
curtains were drawn and the light on – eyewitness accounts

seem to suggest that it had been like that since the Wednesday of her death, and rainwater behind the kitchen door would not have been there unless the door had been left open.

Brian George turned up at about eight-forty-five to do his usual gardening stint and he was to chat with the policeman who told him that the house seemed a bit untidy. Brian George says he found it pretty odd that the policeman had apparently been in the house for two hours without discovering that Hilda Murrell was not there. The policeman said that he then discovered that Hilda Murrell had a relative, a sister-in-law, who lived nearby and he borrowed a duplicate key from her and locked the house up again before going back to police headquarters.

At nine o'clock another gardener arrived. This was David Williams who also worked regularly for Hilda Murrell and the two men began work on the garden. Both remarked that it was odd they had not seen her for a few days and finally decided to go and see if she was all right.

In spite of the policeman's visit, the men found the back door was still open. On the kitchen table were all Hilda's handbags and also her Sizewell papers. The papers were in neat piles. Some drawers were open. There was shopping on the side as if it had been put down by Hilda immediately after coming into the house and on the floor were some rolled-up wet sheets.

The sight of the handbags worried the two men who thought there must have been some kind of a break-in. They called up to Hilda in case she was upstairs but, receiving no reply, assumed she must be in her Welsh bungalow. They decided to ring her there but when they tried to telephone, the line was dead. So they returned to Brian George's house and rang from there only to receive no reply. They returned to the house, this time accompanied by Hilda's cleaning lady, and searched it again. Behind the front door was a pile of newspapers and post. This time they sent for the police.

At first they seem to have given the police the wrong house number, at any event the police first visited 72 Sutton Road instead of 52, but eventually a policewoman and the bearded policeman, who had called in earlier that morning, arrived at the house. At ten twenty Superintendent Needham of the Shrewsbury police arrived.

While this was going on there was other activity elsewhere. At 9 a.m. Rob Green was rung up by his cousin, who lives in Shrewsbury, who told him his aunt seemed to be missing. He rang Hilda's house – there appeared to be no reply. His cousin had told him Hilda's car was missing as well. Even as early as this he felt concerned about the anti-nuclear paper on which his aunt had been working, in view of the fact that she herself had communicated her anxieties over the matter. Green also rang the police.

While police and the two gardeners were waiting in Hilda's house and Rob Green was worrying about his aunt, the police finally began to search the area around where the car had been found. The local policeman, Paul Davies – who had twice reported Hilda's car – called at the home of a local gamekeeper to see if he could help in the search. He was out, but his wife, Chris Randall, was in and she said she would help and gave the policeman a lift in her van. They took her two dogs with them.

They parked near to the abandoned Renault and walked over to the copse, which was the only piece of land nearby in which anything could easily be concealed, and Mrs Randall's dogs almost immediately found Hilda's body.

The body was lying face up and Mrs Randall noted that Hilda's knees were scratched and bloody. There have been several explanations for this – that Hilda had somehow crawled nearly half a mile across a field after being attacked and then died in the copse, that after struggling with her assailant in the car she had been dumped somewhere and then moved to the place where she was found, that she had been dragged or carried from the car unconscious.

She was, as has already been said, only partially clothed.

She was wearing her coat, a pullover and a skirt but no underwear. Her car keys were in the pocket of her coat. There was nothing else near the body. Later the police were to find her hat and a knife, which may have been used to inflict the small stab wounds in her stomach, nearer the road. Her driving licence was found in a hedge and her overshoes were found in a field. One theory is that she might have thrown her belongings around herself to try and attract attention, the other is that her murderer discarded them in a panic.

Back at her house, everybody continued to wait. At ten thirty Superintendent Needham asked Brian George if he might use his telephone to make a 'private' call. Apparently George asked him why he could not use the radio in his car but the superintendent repeated as his reason that the call was a private one. He made the call which was to Detective Chief Superintendent David Cole who told him a body had been found in a copse at Hunkington, presumably that of Hilda Murrell as it fitted her description. The news was then relayed to the people back in Hilda's house.

Towards the end of the morning the police finally contacted Rob Green and told them they had found a body they assumed to be that of his aunt. They could give no cause of death. At first they told him it had been found later than 10.30 a.m., then that it had been discovered at 7 a.m. before finally giving the correct time. There was no explanation for these discrepancies, but in any event her body was found by Mrs Randall's dogs sometime that morning.

As soon as the body was discovered there was a police press release and briefing on the murder, and details began to emerge about the 'ransacked' house, the 'forced entry' by the police and all the other information which was to be revealed by police and interested citizens over the next few days.

Rob Green drove to Shrewsbury and identified his aunt's body. He was shown only the face with its large bruises.

Up to the time of writing he has never been allowed to see any post mortem report in order to know exactly how she died. He was told of the stab wounds but was assured they would not have caused death even in an old lady. He was told that she also had a fractured collar-bone, and this may have been consistent with the jolt when the car came off the road.

So, to summarise the case up to the discovery of the body on March 24th; a burglar entered Hilda Murrell's house. He took out drawers and searched cupboards apparently systematically; disconnected the telephone in a 'professional' manner by removing wires from the junction box using a screwdriver; and was surprised by her return. They struggled; she was injured; a banister rail is knocked out and her assailant abducted her in her white Renault, some six miles across Shrewsbury, where she was later found dead in a copse. He may have been intoxicated, high on drugs or in a state of extreme shock; he was seen driving 'erratically'. A burglary which went wrong or something else? It was, in the words of Lewis Carroll, to become 'curiouser and curiouser'.

THREE

'A Number of Anomalies . . .'

To FOLLOW the stately progress of the police investigation as seen through their briefings and as reported in the press throughout the late spring and summer of 1984 would, taken at face value, give little excuse for the kind of speculation on the Murrell case that has arisen since.

The lady had surprised a burglar who was possibly also a sexual pervert of some kind but who had had time to make a thorough search of her house. She had been abducted, murdered, and her body dumped miles from her home. The police were always on the brink of making an arrest and they endlessly appealed for witnesses. There is not a breath, apart from the one minor report quoted earlier, of the fact that Hilda Murrell had been working up until her death on a paper, on a subject about which the government is highly sensitive, to read at the longest and most controversial public enquiry ever to be held.

As well as the anomalies already mentioned such as the ransacking of the house and the sexual assault, there were a good many others.

After Hilda's body was found it was taken to Shrewsbury Hospital for an immediate post mortem performed by Dr Acland, a Birmingham home office pathologist. As next of kin, Rob Green assumed he would be told what had been discovered and given a copy of the post mortem report but he was refused this point blank and, up until the time of writing, has still not been able to obtain a copy.

When he asked he was told that while he could not be
given the information that was in the report, he could ask
questions about it and the police would try and answer
them.

'You can imagine our difficulties,' he says, 'as since we
had no idea what was on it, we did not know what to
ask.' During a macabre version of Twenty Questions, it
transpired that Hilda Murrell had a broken collar-bone,
small stab wounds in her stomach and probably died of
'hypothermia'. There was definitely no mention of any
kind of sexual assault. In fact, very little was to be revealed
of the details of that post mortem even when the inquest
took place on December 5th. The inquest had already
been postponed twice, first from July 5th to October 24th,
then from October 24th to December 5th.

When Green asked about the disposal of his aunt's body
he was told there could be no question of such at that
stage. It might have to be kept for months, even years, as
it would be needed if the murderer was caught – as it was
expected he would be.

Having accepted what the police told him, Green was
both distressed and very surprised when he was telephoned
on August 3rd by Shrewsbury police and told he must
remove the body straight away as it was deteriorating
rapidly. He was further amazed to be told that a second
autopsy had been carried out, at the request of the police,
on July 25th by a second pathologist, as this might be
needed to provide a second opinion in the event of such
being required by the defence counsel when the murderer
was eventually brought to trial. Green was refused a copy
of this autopsy also.

Green contacted the hospital administrator who confirmed what the police had said, adding that the hospital
authorities would be pleased if Miss Murrell's body could
be removed by August 8th as the space was needed. August
8th was a Sunday and Green asked the hospital to give
him a little more time as it was very short notice, he lived

a considerable distance away and had to arrange matters with an undertaker.

There has never been any adequate explanation as to why the body had to be removed and cremated in such a rush. Why had it deteriorated so badly in the controlled conditions of the mortuary that the police felt impelled to get rid of it? No murderer had been caught. As was to be stated later when the matter of Hilda Murrell's murder finally reached the House of Commons, Helen Smith's dead body survived the sweltering heat of Jeddah and being flown home without deterioration and was then kept in a mortuary for years. (Helen Smith was the British nurse who is alleged to have died following a fall from a balcony during an illegal drinks party in Jeddah. After years of campaigning her father, Ron, finally had an inquest into her death which recorded an open verdict.) Helen's body was subjected to no less than four post mortems and it was the last of these that proved she had been raped before death.

Arrangements were made for the funeral. The body was delivered in a zinc-lined coffin and the family, not surprisingly, were advised not to look inside. On August 25th, 1984, Hilda Murrell was finally cremated.

The anomalies began to come to light. One question which concerned Rob Green was why the police were so slow to follow up the initial report on the finding of his aunt's car in the ditch. All that was needed to discover its owner was for the police to contact the Swansea Drivers and Vehicle Licensing Centre and feed the number into the computer. They told Green that this had, indeed, been done, but that an incorrect number had been fed in and this gave the information that the car had been registered in Scotland and that its owner also lived there.

Towards the end of October I contacted one of the senior police officers involved in the case, Chief Inspector Ferber of the West Mercia police. I had a series of questions to put to him. At first he declined to answer any as the inquest had still not been heard. I pointed out that the matter could hardly be considered *sub judice* as no trial was pending, only the inquest. I asked about the car and why it had not been followed up, about the report by Mr Ian Scott that he had seen no body in the copse and pointed out that surely the police doctor who first examined the body must have been able to tell if it had been moved after death, and raised a number of other items. He declined to answer but later I was rung back by a spokesman on behalf of the chief constable of West Mercia, Robert Cozens.

The statement made to me about the car was that: 'The white Renault car was first seen in the ditch on March 21st by a member of the public who notified the local police. There appeared to be no suspicious circumstances and only superficial damage.' It seems the policeman did take a look. As there appeared to be nothing wrong with the car and it was not causing an obstruction no further action was taken at that time. I asked why not, in view of the fact that the car was not very old and might even have been a stolen one which had already been reported to the police and for which they were looking.

I was told it had been assumed it was an abandoned car. 'Vehicles are abandoned in similar circumstances all over the country. Some 2000 such incidents occur in F division [Shrewsbury] annually. It would be impossible to completely investigate every such incident.' The statement concludes that as the car was still there on March 23rd, the owner was traced which led to the search of Miss Murrell's house on the morning of Saturday March 24th.

So which statement was right? Did the delay caused by feeding a wrong number into the Swansea computer lead to a wild goose chase in Scotland or had the car simply been treated as an uninteresting abandoned vehicle?

The facts speak for themselves. On January 18th, 1985, Tam Dalyell asked the Secretary of State for Scotland if he would call for a report from chief constables in Scotland as to which Scottish police forces were told on Wednesday March 21st, 1984 by the West Mercia police, from details obtained from the DVLC at Swansea, about a white Renault car, number LNT 917W, or other cars abandoned in the Shrewsbury area.

The written reply was: 'I understand there has been no contact between West Mercia constabulary and Scottish police forces about these matters.'

Returning to the finding of the body, I was told that the police had known from the outset that 'one witness' who had visited Moat's Wood (the copse) on the Thursday afternoon after Miss Murrell's death did not see the body which was subsequently found by the police on the morning of March 24th. There was no comment on whether or not the body had been moved. Although if the independent witnesses who spoke to a television journalist are right, and the body was lying in a ditch, then afterwards moved, this is a possibility. Dr Acland, who carried out the post mortem said that it was possible.

Yet surely this fact must have been known, and it would not hinder police enquiries to admit it. It is accepted as standard by forensic pathologists that one of the ways in which time of death is established is to look for hypostasis, or post mortem lividity. It is referred to frequently in Sir Keith Simpson's *Forty Years of Murder* and Sir Keith is the doyen of forensic pathologists. Hypostasis is the draining of the blood to the lowest area of the body when circulation stops. Within six to eight hours the resulting purple stains are fixed. Patches of white skin are, however, left where the body has been in contact with the surface on which it lies and, because of this, it is immediately apparent if a body has been moved after lying for some time in one position.

During the summer-long investigation it became apparent to the brighter souls who were being interviewed that two sets of police were to be involved in the investigation. One was the West Merica police. The other seemed to be the Special Branch. In early September, Hilda Murrell's friend Joan Tate told me, 'The Special Branch are definitely involved somewhere but no one has been told in what way and why and whether they told the local police they were around.' It seems, from talking to people who were involved, that neither set of police seemed properly aware of what the other was doing as some witnesses found out after being interviewed by both.

At first, West Mercia police did not suggest any involvement by the Special Branch. In December 1984, Chief Constable Robert Cozens said that they *had* been involved and that their appearance on the scene was 'a routine measure', since generally speaking local officers support local forces as part of operational procedures.

This prompted a letter in the *Guardian* (January 18th, 1985) which puts the inference of this statement as well as it could be put. Mrs Janet Evans of Woburn in Buckinghamshire wrote: 'I am glad to have Mr Robert Cozens' explanation (*Guardian*, January 10th) of the December/January delay in solving the murder last March of Miss Hilda Murrell.' She continues:

Obviously I'm glad to hear from Mr Cozens (who as chief constable of West Mercia should certainly know) that Special Branch officers were involved in the murder inquiry on a 'routine' basis because of manpower demands; it is good to know that they sometimes spend their time on something more socially useful than bugging my phone.

Now can somebody give me a list of the other 'routine' investigations that Special Branch helped with during 1984 or was this the *only* case with no security implications that they chanced to be involved with?

There is no reason for refusing to give me such a list because, if they were investigating ordinary murders, burglaries and suchlike, the information cannot be classified; and if they helped to solve any of these crimes, it is only right they should have the credit for it to improve their present – rather unfortunate – image.

At every press conference, as has been seen from chapter 1, the police made a good deal of the need for witnesses to come forward and emphasised the hard work, industry and endeavour which were going into the police investigations.

On the first point, there was no shortage of witnesses even if the crucial one, who, the police continually said was sheltering the murderer, did not leap forward. But it did seem rather to depend on the kind of witness you were as to just how the police treated what you had to say.

To quote Joan Tate:

General impressions have been that (a) the police did not even know who Hilda was; (b) did not even know how to pronounce her name (although she and her family firm were immensely well known around here); (c) what is told to the public via the newspapers is not always in keeping with what some of the public know; and (d) the police are not good at handling the more articulate members of the public.

The young man who took my statement . . . wrote that she was always 'kurtius'. Not that spelling matters much, but if they had had tape recorders then perhaps what one actually said could have been transferred to someone who understood from listening. This statement bore very little relation to what I actually said.

One person refused to speak to them and summoned a 'senior officer'. One person, as ex-headmistress of a primary school was asked if she had a nickname. When she enquired why they wished to know such an extraordinary thing, the young constable said that the criminal classes usually did have nicknames.

One witness was described as unreliable and when

further enquiries were made, it turned out to be because
she was a member of CND – a highly respectable lady
I should add.

A number of people who have come forward rather
diffidently with bits of information – as we are all urged
to do, it's called the co-operation of the public – have
been treated extremely offensively and made to seem
foolish. Not the best way to guarantee public co-
operation in future I feel.

She continues, that until the present time she has been
'someone who, on the whole in the past, never had anything to do with the police that has not seemed fair,
sensible, courteous and for the good of the whole, so to
speak'.

So, on to the role of all those policemen. On January
9th, 1985, Mr Tam Dalyell, Labour MP for Linlithgow,
asked Mr Giles Shaw, Minister of State at the Home Office
if he would call for a report from the chief constable of
West Mercia giving the reasons why members of his police
force were suspended before August 1984 during the
course of investigations; when he expected procedures to
be completed; whether they were suspended on full pay
or half pay.

The reply was:

I understand from the chief constable of West Mercia
that on August 7th, 1984 he announced that officers
attached to the No. 4 Regional Crime Squad, were
suspended from duty during the course of an enquiry.
The enquiry began on June 21st, 1984; one officer from
West Mercia and the officer from West Midlands were
suspended on June 28th and the second officer from
West Mercia was suspended on August 2nd. A report
of the enquiry will be submitted to the deputy chief
constable shortly.

In accordance with normal practice the officers were suspended on full pay but one has since resigned from the police service.

At the same time a television researcher was investigating the murder and found that there were a number of suspensions at around the period of the murder enquiry.

Concern grew among Hilda's friends and family that her death might, in some way, be connected with her Sizewell paper, and that her house had been broken into by somebody who wanted to know either what she was planning to say in it, prior to the subsequent cross-examination at Sizewell, or to see if she had got hold of documents she should not have had. But nobody was treated with much sympathy when they asked if Hilda's nuclear research had been taken into account by the police as a possible motive for breaking and entering. The copy of her Sizewell paper found by the police was shown to be a copy with deletions and amendments on it. References in Hilda Murrell's diary show that she had started revising a draft, 'started altering draft', the day before she died. This draft may have been a second copy; we print the clean copy at the end of the book. But any connection between the murder and her paper is still ruled out by the police. Was there any connection between a missing draft and the papers seen on the back seat of her Renault. My own query on this point was answered by the spokesman for the chief constable who said: 'The police have been aware of the various theories suggested and have naturally been prepared to examine any line of enquiry although some will obviously be given more credence than others.' It was known that Miss Murrell was working on a paper which led her into opposition to the Sizewell project and a number of people who might have been able to help on this point had been interviewed by the police. But the police enquiry did not lead them to believe her death was in any way due to her opposition to nuclear power.

The weight of the evidence suggests that it was a burglary which went tragically wrong. On which we all agree.

But there was another reason which was causing growing disquiet, and that was the background of Rob Green himself. He had played what can only be described as a crucial role in the Falklands conflict. As a naval commander, he had acted as personal security adviser to Admiral Sir John Fieldhouse and he was one of a very small number of naval officers who had detailed knowledge of the conduct of that conflict. He worked throughout hostilities at naval headquarters at Northwood in Middlesex and he had been in a position to have known details of exchanges of signals. He had access to signals passing through GCHQ at Cheltenham and, most crucially of all, he probably had detailed knowledge of the signals concerning the *Belgrano*, the sinking of which has become a *cause célèbre*, resulting, among other things in continuous changes of statements right up to the level of the prime minister herself, and the trial of senior civil servant Clive Ponting for passing on classified papers to Tam Dalyell. We will look into both issues, those of the paper on nuclear waste and the *Belgrano* connection, separately.

There has never been any suggestion that Rob Green has acted anything but properly. Anyone who has met him would think it fatuous to consider that he would have removed documents or taken away classified information, but the sinking of the *Belgrano* has produced what can only be described as paranoia in many quarters. Rob Green had begun thinking of early retirement from the navy as early as 1981 for career reasons. As the navy is now organised and with more cutbacks to come, it seemed unlikely he would ever have command of his own vessel and he could therefore see no chance of the kind of promotion he might otherwise have expected. With regard to the Falklands conflict, he had felt the situation should never have been allowed to develop. He knew of the signals which had passed from the Antarctic survey ship, HMS *Endurance*, warning the government that an invasion was likely and still feels that if action had been taken then, the Falklands war would never have happened.

However, once the conflict began he shelved all thought of retirement and worked so well that he was awarded a special citation for his services to this country. He finally left the navy in December 1982 and began working for a local thatcher. He has never deviated from his own view that his aunt's death was in some way connected with the paper on which she had been working.

What leads others apart from Rob Green to think that the break-in at Hilda Murrell's house was something more sinister than a passing burglar? There are a number of reasons.

Firstly, had Hilda Murrell not returned home before going off on her visit to the Drs Symondson in Wales, then anybody breaking in would have had a good long time to search for whatever it was he was looking for. And how would they have found out she was due to be out all day? Quite easily, if her telephone was being tapped.

Anyone who thinks they might be on a tap is accused these days of raging paranoia. Probably most people who think they might be are not. If it is done properly you should not even be aware of it for the days of the heavy breathing policeman sitting shivering in a van, with a notebook and pencil, close to a telegraph pole have long since gone. It should be undetectable but mistakes can occur, and there are instances of strange and repeated faults and noises on lines and even the sound of the voice of the person who owns the phone being played back when they lift the receiver. Noises on the line were put down to tree branches rubbing against telephone wires by the House of Commons' police spokesman, Eldon Griffiths MP, which prompted one wag to suggest they might be

'Special Branches'. But few people believe any home secretary who stands up in the House of Commons and, with
his hand on his heart, says there have been only x number
(usually around 350 to 400) telephone taps authorised by
him in the preceding year and that he is sure, absolutely
sure, that there have been no unofficial taps. It would be
impossible to tell if they *were* unofficial, since no-one
except those involved would be told about them.

To begin with, the whole question of telephone tapping
it shrouded by the all-enveloping 1911 Official Secrets Act,
section 2 of which can cover anything. Telephone tapping
is so secret that no details can be given even to MPs. It is
only supposed to be used in really serious matters – terror-
ism, very serious crime, drug smuggling, and so on and
also in cases involving national security. The latter category
can now mean almost anything however, as we know from
the saga of the series of court cases and appeals involving
the banning of unions at GCHQ, Cheltenham.

But even the assurance that only so many hundred taps
were officially authorised is misleading. For instance, it is
generally assumed that during the 1984/85 miners' strike a
tap was authorised for the NUM. This would not simply
mean that Arthur Scargill's direct line out of the NUM
headquarters in Sheffield could be tapped but the authorisation could also cover all local headquarters and union
offices and even every individual striking miner.

We have no way of knowing if some such blanket authorisation was given to tap the phones of Sizewell objectors
in the name of national security, nor have we any means
of finding out. But if this was the case, then Hilda Murrell
might well have been on a routine tap. If not, then she
could be one of the many people unofficially tapped.
Merlyn Rees, a former Home Secretary, has said that there
may have been such taps – and no-one would know about
them. Likewise, no doubt all those who held important
positions in the services during the Falklands War are kept
under surveillance after they have left the service in which

they were involved and this might also include a telephone tapping. The link therefore between Hilda Murrell and Rob Green was a strong one, possibly with both their lines being tapped. We do not know and we cannot find out.

Tapping today is a sophisticated business carried out by telephone engineers who volunteer to do it and whose work is unknown to their own colleagues. In the older exchanges they will go in at night when nobody is about and, using jump leads, link your number up to a listening centre. This does not need to be local, it is quite easy to monitor you in London if you live in Sheffield – or indeed Shrewsbury. It becomes even easier with the new computerised exchanges which give tappers endless scope, and there is now available equipment so sensitive it can recognise individual voices.

Duncan Campbell revealed in the *New Statesman* in 1982 that there was a centralised tapping centre, known to the police as 'Tinkerbell', situated in Ebury Bridge Road, Chelsea, with a capacity for 1000 lines and employing 200 members of staff. Following his revelation, firstly the name of the place was changed and then the whole operation was moved, probably to a centre in Westminster.

New legislation on telephone tapping is currently being considered by the government not because it actually wants to make changes but because it is being pushed into them. The European Court of Human Rights has condemned current British practice and the House of Lords threatened to throw out the whole Bill privatising British Telecom unless new safeguards were brought in on phone tapping. Just how safe those safeguards will be still remains to be seen.

So it is obvious, from the foregoing, that Hilda's telephone line could easily have been tapped. If this was the case and somebody somewhere did want to have a look around and see what she was working on or if she had documents she should not have had, then the tappers would have had her under surveillance and it would have been known that she was supposed to be going out for the entire day on March 21st. This would give anyone breaking in an uninterrupted period to conduct a search.

Having got in, what then? Well, the obvious thing would be to disconnect the telephone (here the significance of the doctored phone at her Welsh home becomes obvious) before getting down to work.

Had she not come back to leave her shopping and change then possibly nobody would ever have known. A search could have been carried out in such a way that it would have been virtually impossible to tell it had taken place. On the other hand, it could have been made to look like a real burglary with drawers pulled out and their contents tipped on the floor, petty valuables and small items taken and a window forced in an obvious manner.

Strange and unexplained break-ins are not unknown. In 1980, a senior consultant pathologist, Dr Jenny Martin of Chesterfield Royal Infirmary, announced in the *Lancet* that she would be publishing key studies following extensive tests she had carried out on workers involved at the Coalite plant at Bolsover where the controversial herbicide, 245T, had been made. These workers had been contaminated following an explosion there in 1968 which had resulted in a kind of mini-Seveso with 245T, and the contaminant, the deadly dioxin, being released.

A report from the company doctor much quoted by the government when refusing to ban 245T, suggested that the men involved had suffered no ill effects except for the acne-type rash known as chloracne. Dr Martin's research showed the contrary – men had developed problems which included chest and heart trouble and there were signs of changes in their blood.

Dr Martin and her husband, who is also a consultant, live in a detached house in a road of houses in a village near Macclesfield. The position of the house is not unlike that of Hilda Murrell's with a driveway going up to the front door from the road which conceals the house to some extent from passers-by. Immediately next door to the house is her study where files on her work are kept.

She returned home from work shortly after her letter appeared in the *Lancet* to find the folders and files of research on the Coalite workers missing. Nothing else had been touched and there was no obvious sign of a break-in. To this day they have never reappeared and much of the work was irreplaceable. The police, she says, never did take her seriously even when the case reached the national press. They suggested she had 'left it somewhere', lost it at the hospital, the whole inference being that she must be rather eccentric and not know what she did with her things. However, nobody suggested that her study was broken into by a casual burglar and, in the circumstances, it is probably as well that she did not return home early. The case has many similarities to that of Hilda Murrell's.

We will examine, later, who might have been involved in the 'burglary which went tragically wrong'.

On December 5th the inquest on Hilda Murrell was finally held in Shrewsbury, before the coroner, Richard David Clarke. It did not allay the concern of those who attended it.

The only witnesses called were Detective Chief Superintendent Cole and the Home Office pathologist, Dr Peter Acland. Dr Acland described in some detail the injuries to the body. They included a broken collar-bone, a blow to the face, wounds to the stomach, bruising around the hyoid and thyroid cartilages and so on. (In cases of strangulation it is usual for the hyoid cartilage to be broken but as there was no evidence of asphyxia the coroner says, discussing this case, that the damage was consistent with 'mugging by the arm of the assailant'.)

Death, in his opinion, was due to hypothermia and penetrating wounds to the abdomen with multiple bruises to the face. He felt there was some evidence that she had been crawling. 'I cannot be certain that she died in the exact spot where she was found but she could have died up to a hundred yards away but within that area. It is not possible to say when she died but in my opinion I would have thought she died between five and ten hours after being abandoned. In my opinion it is likely that she died on March 21st, 1984.'

He went on to say it was not his decision to ask for a second post mortem but 'Dr Gower who carried out the second post mortem . . . entirely agreed with all my findings and conclusions.' No new evidence had come to light. Questioned as to the hypostasis he said it was 'usually' a good indication that the body had not been moved after death as it takes some hours for it to develop, 'so that it is a possibility that within a few minutes after death it could have been moved, but I would have thought that if it had been any longer than an hour or so after death, then the changes in this hypostasis would have indicated to me that there had been some interference after death'. Hypostasis in some areas was 'faint'.

There was no evidence of sexual assault. He thinks Hilda Murrell was possibly 'frogmarched' across the field but 'I can't say this with any great degree of certainty.' The injuries to the knees were 'I think, due to her crawling around . . . The abrasions on her knees could have been consistent with her being dragged. . . . I can't exclude that she might have been dragged.'

The bruise on her face appeared to be

. . . a broad blunt impact. Because of its broad nature, I think it is less likely to have been caused by a fist, a kick is probably more likely, although there was a car accident, so I think we must bear in mind that some of the injuries may be due to this. As I understand it, there were no blood stains on the window of the car, but I'm not certain about this so the kick is probably the strongest possibility of the options.

The police say the accident to the car was a 'slight one'.

Regarding the stab wounds, he said that 'a blood stained handkerchief was found in the right pocket of her coat, which was adjacent to the stab wounds, but I am not sure whether the handkerchief was stained because of this or whether she used the handkerchief to mop up some earlier injury. I can't remember the exact proximity of the pocket to the knife wounds.' Numerous 'punctuate erosions were noted in the mucosa and this is a feature consistent with hypothermia'.

The coroner then told the inquest that it was his duty after the first post mortem to retain the body so that when a person had been charged they could have their own post mortem carried out in order properly to conduct their defence. However, he had been advised that as the body was deteriorating rapidly it would shortly be impractical for a second post mortem to be carried out if somebody was eventually charged, and so a second one was authorised to take place immediately which could be made available to the defence. He did not explain why the body had been allowed to deteriorate in such a way and why it had not been refrigerated in view of the fact that a murder investigation was still under way.

Cole then gave his evidence. He began by saying that while he was prepared to disclose as much evidence as possible to assist the inquest 'I am not prepared to disclose all evidence in my possession. This is in no way an attempt to conceal anything, but I must be in a position to put evidence to a suspect which has not previously been re-leased so that the accuracy of anything a suspect tells me may be tested.'

He then described the finding of the body and a detailed description of what it looked like. He also said that Hilda's car was a short distance away where it appeared 'to have come to rest after a slight accident'. Officers, he said, had attended the vehicle within a hour of its first being reported as being there but, he repeated, as there appeared to be nothing wrong 'at that stage they took no action'. As the car was still there on the Friday, enquiries were instituted and a search made on the Saturday morning.

Cole then described the state of the house and what he imagined had happened, how Hilda had come back from shopping and disturbed a burglar, who, after attacking her, drove her in an erratic manner to where her car was found. 'The police have been aware from the outset that one witness, Mr Scott, has stated that he was in the Moat Wood at approximately 3.30 p.m. on March 22nd, 1984, and that he did not see Miss Murrell's body. This has been carefully considered and researched. He may be mistaken. The body was in a slight hollow and dressed in clothing which matched the undergrowth.' Intensive enquiries had taken place and some 3,590 persons nominated as potential suspects checked out.

Cole went on to say that certain newspapers and individuals had suggested that Miss Murrell's death may be connected with her views which were opposed to the use of nuclear power/arms. They had drawn attention particularly to the fact that she was, at the time of her death, preparing a paper to oppose the Sizewell B project.' Being aware of this, this aspect was looked into.

A small team of officers was specifically assigned to enquire into the Sizewell B aspect but has failed to find any evidence connecting this project with Miss Murrell's death or, for that matter, her view on any other matters connected with nuclear arms. In fact, this morning, I have reviewed all the evidence at my disposal both photographic and film, and I am still left with the inescapable conclusion that this was an offence of burglary and that the offender was in the main after cash. There is evidence contained within my incident room which leads to that conclusion.

As has been noted, the pathologist found no evidence of sexual assault. Cole said: 'Subsequent forensic tests revealed she had been subjected to some form of sexual activity.' As we will see when we come to the statement made by Giles Shaw, the police denied that there had been any sexual assault or interference with Hilda Murrell and went further by suggesting this was not something that had ever been said by them. Yet on April 9th Cole himself had given a statement to the press in which he categorically stated that Hilda Murrell had been the object of a sexual assault. This is just another of the many discrepancies between the inquest evidence, what had been said before and what was to be said later in Giles Shaw's statement of police evidence in reply to Tam Dalyell's questions in the House of Commons.

Cole was asked only *two* questions. On the injuries to Hilda Murrell and where they were inflicted he said: 'Had the injuries caused to Miss Murrell been inflicted in her own home, we would have expected to find evidence in the house. I can't say that the injuries were definitely inflicted within the coppice, but somewhere between the car and the coppice.' No, had it been found that there was some connection with her death and her work in the anti nuclear field, 'we would not have felt in any way inhibited in our enquiries.' Police enquiries were still going on.

The coroner then said he found the causes of death to be hypothermia, and stab wounds to the abdomen with multiple bruising to the face. Therefore his verdict was that the deceased was killed unlawfully.

The inquest begs many questions. Why, if Ian Scott 'may' be wrong about the body not being there on the Thursday but could not positively be proved to be so, was he not called as a witness? Indeed, why were there no other witnesses called at all! And surely, if the police held evidence that showed, beyond a shadow of doubt, that the motive for the break-in and attack was petty robbery, then it would obviously be sensible to publish it and thus quell all speculation once and for all. It would be unlikely to prejudice the outcome of any subsequent trial.

On a *World in Action* programme on Hilda Murrell transmitted on March 4th, Dr Acland, while stressing that he personally thought it unlikely her body had been moved from where it first lay, said that the hypostasis he found on it did not altogether rule it out. He called his first view 'Option 1'. 'Option 2 presents much more difficulty,' he told the reporter. 'It would require two people to move her with great care and then to replace her in exactly the same position as she had lain before but – no – it can't be ruled out.'

It would appear that both the coroner and Mr Giles Shaw in his reply of January 17th, 1985 were incorrect when it came to the decision not to allow the family a copy of the post mortem report. Mr Shaw had said: 'Turning to the availability to Miss Murrell's family of the post mortem report, the release of this on formal application is a matter entirely within the coroner's discretion and not one in which I would intervene.'

Inquest, the United Campaign for Justice, says: 'The supply of a post mortem report on formal application is covered by Rule 57 of the Coroners Rules 1984 (S.I. No. 552). These Rules do not, however, apply to a post mortem conducted before July 1st 1984 and the relevant Rule is therefore Rule 39 of the Coroners Rules 1953 (S.I. No. 205). Both these rules include the following words:

A coroner *shall* on application and on payment of the prescribed fee (if any) supply to any person who, in the opinion of the coroner, is a properly interested person a copy of any report of a post mortem examination . . .

'The release of the post mortem is *not* then 'entirely within the coroner's discretion' once he has decided that the applicant is a 'properly interested person'. The phrase 'properly interested person' is also used to describe a person who is entitled to question witnesses at an inquest. It is very difficult to see how a coroner can acknowledge a person as 'properly interested' in being represented at an inquest, but not in applying for a copy of the post mortem. We would argue that it is not within the coroner's lawful discretion to withhold the post mortem report from a person who is entitled to examine witnesses at inquest, as defined by rule 20 of the 1984 Rules. And so the family were entitled to receive a copy of the report, which might have gone some way to explaining the circumstances of Hilda Murrell's death. The disclosure of a report could not prejudice investigations – if these really were proceeding as police statements indicated.

FOUR

The Nuclear Connection

BEFORE TAKING Hilda Murrell's story any further, it is
necessary to look at the two possible reasons for the
break-in to her house. The first is the nuclear connection.

Section 2 of the 1911 Official Secrets Act covers just
about everything from what kind of lavatory paper is used
in the Ministry of Defence to minor memos about tea-ladies
handed around at the Treasury. It also covers more important matters such as anything to do with nuclear energy
that either the government or the industry does not want
you to know – which is just about everything.

Yet no matter how many advertising agencies are called
in to explain that nuclear power is absolutely, perfectly
safe and really is good for you, the general public seems
to remain suspicious. Reassurances of that perfect safety
and thousands of words about the foolproof operating
standards of British Nuclear Fuel's plant at Sellafield (ex-
Windscale) tend to sound a little thin as stories of clusters
of leukaemia patients around nuclear power stations and
publicity about continual accidents, leaks and problems at
Sellafield continue to receive national publicity. All this
came to a head in the autumn of 1983 when, as a result of
the activities of the organisation Greenpeace who were
trying to block up the waste discharge pipe from Sellafield
into the Irish Sea, it was discovered that miles of Cumbrian
beaches were contaminated with radiation.

It was in October 1979, only five months after taking

office, that the Prime Minister held a meeting of the
Cabinet Committee on economic strategy at 10 Downing
Street. It was a select group of ministers – Lord Carrington,
Sir Keith Joseph, James Prior, Michael Heseltine, Sir
Geoffrey Howe, David Howell, Peter Walker, John Nott
and John Biffen, with George Younger and the Attorney
General, Sir Michael Havers, also in attendance. The
subject was the new government's nuclear power policy.

Mrs Thatcher put it over in the strongest terms that she
wanted to embark on a massive programme of building
ten pressurised water nuclear reactors (PWRs) in ten years
starting then. The Committee knew there were some problems. Unfortunately the design chosen was very similar to
that involved in the notorious Three Mile Island accident
in the United States about which one headline read 'The
Night We Nearly Lost Pennsylvania'.

It was recognised even at that early stage that there
could be a few problems with public opinion. There were,
read the Cabinet minutes (classified 'Secret') 'substantial
problems in achieving nuclear programmes. Opposition to
nuclear power might well provide a focus for protest groups
over the next decade and the government might make
more rapid progress towards its objective by a low profile
approach . . .', but there would be a problem in maintain-
ing a low profile once a decision was made to proceed with
the PWR – because of Three Mile Island.

The result was the decision to go ahead with PWR 1 and
the site chosen was at Sizewell, on the Suffolk coast, next
to a present Magnox type nuclear reactor. The public
enquiry held, one feels in part as a public relations exercise,
has – at the time of writing – lasted for two years. Millions
of words have been transcribed and presented at it, hundreds of witnesses have taken part, it has cost the Central
Electricity Generating Board (CEGB) (that is you, the
taxpayer) at least ten million pounds, probably considerably more.

It seems the CEGB is pretty sure of the outcome,

however, as it has already ordered components for the PWR ready for when it has been given the go-ahead.

People remain ambivalent about nuclear power. They are told it is relatively cheap. Yet there are reports which prove it is both expensive and inefficient. Which should they believe? They are told it is safe and that there are no provable cases of people being harmed by living near nuclear power stations. Yet perhaps there is something odd about those leukaemia cases at Sizewell, near Winfrith in Dorset and at Seascale, near Sellafield in Cumbria. But you can't prove anything.

However, on the question of nuclear waste there is no controversy at present for nobody has yet found a safe way to dispose of it. All nuclear power stations produce nuclear waste and PWRs produce a variety which is particularly difficult to handle. If the waste is left on site then what happens as it accumulates? If you transfer it up to Sellafield, as happens at the moment, then it is at risk while it is in transit. Then what *do* you do with it? Storage facilities are simply running out.

At the end of the life of a nuclear power station it has to be 'decommissioned' – that is, made safe – not just for the immediate future but for thousands of years. Here we are talking really big money. Nobody knows quite how to set about it anyway, but it can be confidently stated that any method embarked upon would be very, very expensive. Even the CEGB revealed in its annual report for 1981 (*New Scientist*, August 5th, 1982) that at that time it would cost at least two hundred and seventy million pounds to decommission a small Magnox station.

Whenever it is found that strange men with surveying equipment are wandering around a locality and word gets about that they are looking for suitable storage sites for nuclear waste, there is a public outcry. Nobody wants it near them. In 1983, two favoured sites were announced (or rather admitted to) by the Department of the Environment, one in old underground mines beneath land owned by ICI at Billingham in Cleveland and the other at Elstow in Bedfordshire.

The Billingham option brought about the most remarkable alliance composed of all the inhabitants of Billingham, all the political parties in the area, every type of environmental and amenity group and, in the end, ICI itself who refused to allow surveyors into the mines even to look at the site. This really did put the lid on the scheme and, faced with such intransigence, on January 25th, 1985 the government gave in and the environment minister, Patrick Jenkin, announced in the House of Commons that Billingham was no longer considered suitable as a site.

There were, however, six other sites under consideration. One of these puts the spotlight on unfortunate Elstow, very near to sizeable conurbations and where a well-organised protest movement is working hard. One of its debates with the waste dumpers was televised in the autumn of 1984 by Central Television. The argument there has become, literally, bogged down in details as to how deep the surveyors drilled into the London clay and why much of the information given as to the suitability of the site keeps changing.

Anxieties about carrying nuclear waste from the different and far flung nuclear power stations to Sellafield in Cumbria for reprocessing has also led to more anxiety, this time relating to just how safe the process is and what would happen if a train carrying the containers for the waste, known as 'flasks', had a serious accident – there have already been a number of minor ones. For plutonium rods from nuclear power stations are actually far more dangerous on their return journey after use than when they arrived to do their work, for the plutonium has been broken down into a number of other elements, some of which are very dangerous, indeed lethal. Just one of them, ruthenium, is so dangerous that one thirty-millionth of a gramme in a lung would cause a person to suffer a fatal lung cancer.

There was a good deal of criticism about the strength of the flasks used to transport the waste, whether there was any leakage and if they would withstand a real impact without breaking open or bursting into flames. The flasks used by the CEGB until recently had never been tested in real conditions: trials for safety had always been carried out on half-sized models.

With the issue of nuclear waste becoming ever more controversial, the CEGB decided to stop the flask controversy once and for all, and in the summer of 1984 staged a spectacular train crash – at a cost to the taxpayer of four million pounds – designed to show everybody, in detail and on television, that even a 100 mph train crash could not possibly harm a flask carrying nuclear waste.

Unfortunately, confidence in this stunning event was undermined when, on October 23rd, 1984, the environmental group Greenpeace released documents which they claimed showed the train crash as 'a giant public relations confidence trick rigged by the CEGB' (*Guardian*, October 23rd, 1984). The allegations made by Greenpeace were that the papers leaked to them showed that the train crash was not the worst that could happen to a flask, it was the least bad of seven proposed scenarios, but the most spectacular, which is why it had been chosen. It was chosen to ensure the flask remained intact.

The engineers who had leaked the report to Greenpeace claimed that bolts had been taken out of the locomotive so that it was less rigid on impact and that concrete blocks had been piled in the carriages to lessen secondary impact which had been identified by the CEGB's own engineers as increasing the dangers of the flasks being broken open on impact. The locomotive used was a type 46, the engineers had stated that types 47, 50 and 87 were much more likely to cause trouble. The CEGB admitted the leaked documents were genuine but said their findings were now out of date.

Dumping waste at sea had stopped by the middle of

1984, not because many other countries were objecting to Britain's sea dumping but because the National Union of Seamen refused to keep on doing it. In the autumn of 1984 even the government agreed not to dump any more solid waste in the sea until further investigations had been carried out.

It was also announced that the amount of nuclear waste going into the Irish Sea from British Nuclear Fuel's plant at Sellafield was to be severely cut back following the appalling press BNF had received over the contamination of the Cumbrian beaches in the autumn of 1983. The amount of nuclear waste which has poured into the Irish Sea since BNF began discharging its waste there has led to that sea being called the dirtiest sea in the world and a report published in May 1982 showed that Sellafield was up to 1000 times 'dirtier' than its nearest rival, Cap de la Hague on the French coast.

The best summation of the question of nuclear waste is still that from the 1976 Royal Commission on Environmental Pollution chaired by Lord Flowers which says: 'There should be no commitment to a large programme of nuclear fission power until it has been demonstrated beyond reasonable doubt that a method exists to ensure the safe containment of long-lived, radioactive waste for the indefinite future.' The Labour Government of the day responded to this, saying that '. . . the Commission's proposition is bound to be the dominant factor in any process preceding decisions about further large-scale programmes.'

Apart from anything else, the sheer cost of the disposal of the nuclear waste and, even more important, the decommissioning of nuclear power stations after their life has ended, is a hot political potato. The CEGB did not even begin to make provision for decommissioning its nuclear power stations until April 1976, although there had been stations in operation since the early 1960s. In 1978/79 the CEGB set the sum of twenty million pounds aside to cover the cost of decommissioning its then nine nuclear power stations and making the redundant and waste material safe. In 1980/81 the sum was increased to thirty million pounds. Currently the CEGB gives no estimate. To put that figure more into real terms, the current estimated cost for decommissioning the no. 2 reactor at Three Mile Island is put at more than one billion dollars . . . That is for one reactor in one power station.

So it is against this highly political background that Hilda Murrell began researching her Ordinary Citizen's View, the most sensitive aspect of the whole nuclear power programme and the one area where most of what its critics have to say, remains *unanswerable*. To date, there is *no* satisfactory method for the disposal of nuclear waste.

Her paper (published at the end of this book) is in fact a detailed attack on the government's own White Paper on Radioactive Waste Management and in her opening remarks she says something which was to become all too significant. Talking of the White Paper she says:

> The last sentence reads: 'Throughout, the public must be kept fully informed about what is being done, and there must be proper scope for public discussion.' Hear. Hear. The whole nuclear enterprise was started, and has continued, in closely guarded secrecy, and hundreds of millions of pounds of Ordinary Citizens' money has been spent on it without their knowledge, let alone consent, or Parliament being involved at all. Only little by little has it been possible for them to realise the extent of this commitment and the seriousness of the issues raised by it. That such a thing could be done in a democratic society on a matter of such importance is highly disturbing. The Ordinary Citizen is entitled to complete frankness from now on.

She then went to town on some of the assertions made in the White Paper such as 'One basic characteristic of radioactivity, which actually assists in waste management, is that it decays over time.' Indeed, she says, 'It is precisely the "decay" of unstable elements which *is* the radioactive event, and which therefore poses all the ensuing problems. To say that decay "actually assists in waste management" is to stand the whole situation on its head and is unbelievably fatuous.' As she continues, 'The bright and cheery thought conveyed by the quotation is as pure an example of "newspeak" as could be found. Windscale into Sellafield is another. The deep mental dishonesty they betray is terrifying.'

Hilda latched on to two points worth mentioning here in her reasoned attack on the financial, technical and environmental problems of dealing with nuclear waste. She was obviously concerned at the pollution of the Cumbrian beaches the preceding autumn. She says:

> There is now a quarter of a ton of plutonium in the Irish Sea. It would be beyond belief had it not happened, that it could ever have been thought permissible to throw out this stuff into the living environment without any proper scientific examination of the results of such action. Even if the totally unjustified assumption that it would remain conveniently stuck in the sediments on the seabed had been correct, had they never heard of the habit of plaice and other flatfish of lying precisely there?

After criticising all those involved who had defended the disposal of waste at Sellafield she says that exactly what the objectors to this method have said all along has now happened '. . . and this has been shown up, not by the "regulatory bodies", but by a band of heroic amateurs, who were promptly fined fifty thousand pounds for their efforts to protect us. There has been either a total failure to monitor the place properly, or else eyes have been deliberately closed so that costs of waste treatment should not become an embarrassment to the industry.'

Concerned as she was with secrecy and its effects on democracy, she makes a point concerning the 'nuclear police' who will be looked at in more detail (so far as it is possible) in the chapter on the security services. Expressing her misgivings about this special and secret force she says: 'This police force is almost certainly paid for by the Secret Service, to which technically it belongs, and the real cost of nuclear power is thus reduced.'

When she reaches her conclusions at the end of the document she describes the government White Paper as '. . . depressing. The frequent expressions in it of the government's "beliefs", "convictions" and "considered judgements" are contradicted by the facts which are glaring.' She describes the efforts of the government and the nuclear industry to disguise the facts about the disposal of nuclear waste as likely to tax a 'super-Machiavelli'.

She ends:

The inescapable burden now inflicted on posterity imposes a straight moral choice, which was not faced in the beginning but which must be faced now. Even a desperate need for energy would not justify creating these worst of all pollutants, whose control for merely a few centuries (in the case of high level waste) we cannot guarantee, far less that of the long-life actinides which are forever. We have not even a moderate need for this technology, never mind a desperate one.

This is a failed and dying industry, which is a major liability and should be closed down. The fact that plans can be made for adding to it shows an unbelievable degree of irresponsibility and stupidity in all concerned.

The Ordinary Citizen implores the director to urge the right moral choice on the government, which should redirect all its spare billions towards energy conservation, cleaning up fossil-fuelled power stations and developing alternative energy sources.

But well reasoned as it is, there is nothing actually new in Hilda Murrell's paper. She did not have access to leaked documents or information being withheld from the public – so far as we are aware. What she needed to know could be discovered from a variety of reports published both here and in the United States – where, of course, the 1976 Freedom of Information Act allows far more access by the 'ordinary citizen' and anybody else to such information.

What she had done was provide a paper which could easily be assimilated by anybody who had an interest in the subject and which would, no doubt, be of use to groups up and down the country who could find themselves fighting proposals to dump nuclear waste on their door-steps.

There is some evidence that she was worried about the cross-examination which would follow her reading of the paper at Sizewell and had enquired to see if somebody might read her paper for her, not because she was frightened or felt she could not cope but simply because of the considerable physical effort which would be involved. She was told she would have to present it and be cross-examined in person and to this she had resigned herself.

So, we have a situation where an intelligent lay person has prepared a paper to be read at the Sizewell enquiry on a subject which is supersensitive. If, as we have already discussed, it was possible that as an objector her telephone had already been tapped and it it was decided by somebody somewhere that it would be useful to find out exactly what it was she was going to say, then it would be in the interest of those concerned to take a look and find out. If nothing else, it would strengthen the hand of the cross-examiner when it came to the enquiry.

If we add the *Belgrano* connection, then the desire to know just what was in her house would become irresistible.

FIVE

The Belgrano *Connection*

WHEN THE twelve 'ordinary people' acquitted senior civil servant Clive Ponting on February 11th, 1985 and refused to find him guilty under the notorious section 2 of the 1911 Official Secrets Act they were doing more than just returning a simple verdict, however surprising the verdict. They were sending a definite message to those who had brought the prosecution and to the government, which was behind it, that the prosecution should never have been brought and that they had agreed with Clive Ponting, that it was utterly wrong that ministers of the Crown should deliberately seek to mislead the House of Commons over the events surrounding the sinking of the Argentine cruiser, *General Belgrano*, in May 1982.

The verdict was returned in the teeth of all kinds of difficulties from the vetting of the jury by the Special Branch to a restrictive interpretation of the law necessary to convict. Not only that, but had they returned a verdict of guilty, they would have been upholding the very doubtful doctrine which was expressed in the words of Mr Justice McCowan during his summing up—

Only one ingredient of the charge is in dispute – whether what Ponting did was 'his duty in the interests of the State'. The prosecution say, where is there a scintilla of evidence it was his official duty?

I direct you this means 'the policies of the State' as they were in July 1984 and not the policies of the State as Ponting, Tam Dalyell, you or I think they ought to have been. It is not a question of the Conservative Party being the State. It is not a political matter at all. The policies of the State were the policies of the Government then in power.

The jury disagreed. It was, from the start, a deeply political matter and the jury agreed with Ponting that duty to the State meant duty to the Crown in Parliament, not to a government concerned only with saving its own political face.

It has been necessary to put this into the story of Hilda Murrell as it is an essential part of the second thread of the story of the break-in – government paranoia over anything whatsoever to do with the sinking of the *Belgrano*, and the frantic search throughout 1983 and most of 1984 for leaked documents which had anything to do with the period in question.

This is not the place to go into the rights and wrongs of the decision to sink the *Belgrano*. But there has been controversy ever since over the necessity to sink an old Second-World-War cruiseship (she had survived Pearl Harbour) some fifty miles outside what the government had declared to be the Total Exclusion Zone and when she was sailing for home.

The cover-up, the frantic searches for documents and the misleading not only of the House of Commons in general but the Commons' Select Committee in particular, date back to May 4th, 1982 when Sir John Nott, then defence minister, stood up in the House and made a statement on the *Belgrano* and its sinking with the loss of 368 lives. 'This heavily armed surface attack group', he said of the ageing *Belgrano* and its two accompanying destroyers, 'was close to the Total Exclusion Zone and was closing on elements of our Task Force which was only hours away . . .'

There had been a gradual decline in the standards of accuracy and consistency required of Parliamentarians and we had reached a stage when it was easy, whether intentionally or not, to produce misleading information.

It transpired that not only was the *Belgrano* not closing in on the Task Force but that the prime minister's early statements, that the government and war cabinet had been unaware of the presence of the *Belgrano* until May 2nd, 1982, were wrong also. As the commander, Wreford-Brown, was to state later: 'We located her [the *Belgrano*] on our passive sonar, and sighted her visually on the afternoon of May 2nd. We took up a position astern and followed the *Belgrano* for over thirty hours. We reported that we were in contact with her.'

For over two years MP Tam Dalyell had been persistently questioning the government on the *Belgrano* issue, often to the annoyance and exasperation of his own Labour benches. He has wanted to know why the *Belgrano* was sunk. His own view, which is not held by all the other critics of the sinking and certainly not by all those who have intensely disliked government policy on the releasing of information on the subject, is that the ship was sunk quite deliberately to scupper the Peruvian peace initiative which would have prevented all out physical war between Britain and Argentina. Certainly it led to direct retaliation on HMS *Sheffield* and the subsequent loss of British lives.

A good deal of Dalyell's persistent questioning and the subsequent non answers have been directly concerned with the times at which events took place, most particularly the sending of signals back and forth between the submarine HMS *Conqueror* and the naval headquarters at Northwood in Middlesex. The commander of HMS *Conqueror*, Commander Wreford-Brown, was later to state on several occasions that he received the signal to sink the *Belgrano* at 3 p.m. on May 2nd. He also states that he actually

queried the signal which suggests that he himself had
doubts over what it was he was being asked to do. However, having received confirmation, he obeyed his orders.

Here, again, wild discrepancies arise. The government
consistently said that there was difficulty and delay in
the sending and receiving of signals between the naval
headquarters at Northwood and the Task Force and this
has also been put forward as one reason for the delay in
actually ordering the sinking of the *Belgrano*. If, as it now
transpires, the *Belgrano* had been miles outside the Total
Exclusion Zone and steaming away, yet had been followed
for thirty hours when she was much nearer to the Task
Force, surely she should have been attacked earlier had
it been necessary to do so for the safety of our ships?
Commander Wreford-Brown has, however, always denied
that there were signalling delays, saying that the system
was 'working well' at the time at which he received the
signal to sink the *Belgrano*.

It has also become apparent that GCHQ at Cheltenham
had not only been passing on signals to Northwood but
had been intercepting and decoding virtually all the signals
between the Argentinian command and its own fleet.
GCHQ had known the *Belgrano* was on her way home.

Signal activity at Northwood was intense and constant
and it is therefore obvious that Commander Rob Green,
Hilda Murrell's nephew, working as he was at Northwood
throughout the Falklands War and in constant contact
during those crucial days leading up to the sinking of the
Belgrano with what was going on and the signals passing
to and fro, must have been in possession of a good deal of
highly secret and crucial information. It would be surprising, therefore, if he had not been kept under some kind
of surveillance once he had left the service in the December
of that same year even though he had firmly stated that he
wished to leave the navy before the Falklands War had
been a possibility.

So, by the early part of 1983 he was settled in Dorset

learning to be a thatcher and Hilda Murrell was beginning to assemble the information and evidence to go into her Sizewell paper. They were in touch mainly by telephone. It was during that period that Labour MP Tam Dalyell began his persistent questioning in Parliament on the true sequence of events surrounding the sinking of the Argentinian cruiser.

Long before the sensational arrest of senior civil servant Clive Ponting in the summer of 1984, it had become apparent that Dalyell was getting hold of accurate information from somewhere and it must be stressed that it was by no means coming in the early part of 1984 from Clive Ponting. Dalyell had other high-up sources as well. One of these sources told him that during the period of December 19th/20th, 1983 a special enquiry was set up under Sir Robert Armstrong, Secretary to the Cabinet, to investigate urgently leaks relating both to GCHQ at Cheltenham – and there had been plenty of dissatisfaction there following the government's decision in 1984 to ban trade unions at GCHQ – and into the sinking of the *Belgrano*. Various people were to be 'checked out' and the security services were involved in this checking.

Dalyell's source was to tell him there was 'a tremendous flap in Downing Street' at the beginning of March 1984 and this seemed to be supported by the evidence given by Defence Minister Michael Heseltine, to the House of Commons Select Committee on Foreign Affairs in the autumn of 1984.

It had partly been triggered off by a letter from Labour's Defence spokesman, Denzil Davies MP on March 6th, 1984. The letter asked one simple question – was the *Belgrano* first sighted on May 1st or 2nd? It was as a direct result of this letter – to the Prime Minister not to Mr Heseltine – that Heseltine commissioned the document on the sinking of the *Belgrano* which was to become known as 'The Crown Jewels', a document which contained information far too secret to be revealed to Parliament or the

Select Committee but which could freely be shown to the twelve jurors at the trial of Clive Ponting – when it suited the government to do so.

Heseltine commissioned the document, which was written by Clive Ponting, in anticipation of top level meetings. One of these was so urgent that it had necessitated a discussion between Heseltine and the Prime Minister on the evening before the Minister had flown off to Germany on urgent NATO business.

Intelligence and the security services were told to do everything possible to identify the origin of the leaks of information about the *Belgrano* and certainly that must have included any possible leaks on what were described as 'raw signals', the originals of which were supposed to have been destroyed following the end of hostilities in the South Atlantic. It might also, one imagines, have included a search for the missing helmsman's log from the *Conqueror*, a loss which was not to be made public until Heseltine gave his evidence to the House Select Committee in the autumn of 1984. Half the time we have been told it is unimportant and not top secret while the rest of the time has been spent frantically trying to find it because of what it might contain.

According to Tam Dalyell and his source, it was at this stage that the security services decided 'to take a look' at Rob Green as they were under intense pressure to come up with something from somewhere. As Dalyell was later to tell the House of Commons on December 20th, 1984, 'He came under a cloud of suspicion, wrongly to the best of my knowledge . . .' It was thought he might have copies of documents or even raw signals, some of the originals of which had been destroyed by the intelligence services – so Dalyell's source alleged.

It is indeed ironic that there was such paranoia over raw signals, back at the beginning of March 1984, which may or may not have gone missing like the log.

It has been suggested that the signals traffic which had

been intercepted by GCHQ at Cheltenham may have shown that the *Belgrano* had never entered the Total Exclusion Zone at all and that she had neither sailed for, nor attempted to, attack the Task Force. It has also been reported that the so-called 'pincer movement' so often described by ministers – i.e. the combined threat of attack from the aircraft carrier, the *25 De Mayo* and the *General Belgrano* – was something which appeared to be mere speculation from the naval headquarters at Northwood. There appears to have been no evidence of signals from the Argentine government telling the *Belgrano* to attack the Task Force.

Mrs Thatcher's War Cabinet did not receive the signals themselves but the signals as summarised and interpreted by the naval intelligence staff at Northwood where the 'pincer theory' was born. So, at the beginning of March 1984 when only a limited amount had come out about the *Belgrano* affair it seems that there were a limited number of people who knew what had been in those raw signals intercepted by GCHQ Cheltenham.

The view which Dalyell was to put forward to the House and which will be dealt with in more detail in the next chapter, was that while it was pretty widely known that people who had leaked documents would be unlikely to keep them in their own homes (neatly filed under 'leaks', perhaps, for easy access?), they might well have involved friends and relations in holding information for them. It was not surprising in view of the sensitivity of the *Belgrano* issue and that Rob Green was one of only two officers from Northwood who had left the navy following the Falklands War, that suspicion might have fallen on him in view of the crucial nature of the role he had played during the conflict.

If Dalyell is, therefore, correct in his allegation that there was a very definite link between Rob Green – however innocent – and the possible desire of the security services to find out if he had taken anything, then they might well have looked around to see where he might have concealed information. A quick check of his close friends and relatives would have revealed that Hilda Murrell was his aunt and, lo and behold! the lady was already on file for her anti nuclear activities.

Their link in the minds of those who think like MI5 and the Special Branch would be an immediate one. Here was a woman known to be against government policy on certain issues, working in a field which was deeply sensitive and involved in activities, which to some people, could be considered as anti State.

According to Mr Justice McCowan's summing up in the Ponting trial, democratic dissent from and legitimate activity against, the government policy of the day could actually be construed as being not just anti that government or that particular policy but actually anti State and against the interests of national security. Since this also appears to be an opinion currently held in government circles, then presumably this could have been the line of reasoning behind any authorisation for a break-in to Hilda Murrell's home.

If Hilda Murrell disagreed with the nuclear power programme then she might well have disagreed with the Falklands War in general, and the sinking of the *Belgrano* in particular. Why not? If her telephone was tapped, as seems extremely likely, then it would have been known she was in touch with the Morgan Grenvilles and EcoRopa. And EcoRopa had not only published leaflets against nuclear power they had also published a leaflet deeply critical of the Falklands War.

So who might her nephew turn to if he was dissatisfied also and had illegally taken away information and documents he should not have had? Why, to his aunt of course. As Rob Green says, even if he had taken away anything he should not – and there was never the slightest question that he would have done any such thing – then the last thing he would have done would be to have put a close relative at risk by leaving such documents around in her house. The security services might at least have given him some credit for common sense, he having spent his career in naval intelligence.

The general panic and changing of stories and misleading of the House of Commons went on throughout the rest of 1984. It led to the arrest and charging of Clive Ponting under section 2 of the 1911 Official Secrets Act and his subsequent trial in January/February 1984. Goodness only knows what kind of security searches went on during 1984, who was under surveillance and who undertook it, during a period of such feverish activity. We know now, from allegations made in a Channel 4 programme on MI5, what people suspected – that tapping and mail tampering had actually taken place, the targets being members of a group actively dissenting from the government's nuclear policies. The allegations suggested that MI5 officers had exceeded their brief. The *Belgrano* issue quite simply refused to go away.

Whether the break-in at Hilda Murrell's house was brought about because of the 'flap' over leaked *Belgrano* documents, whether it was because of her nuclear connection or whether it was a combination of both remains to be discovered – possibly years in the future – but there is no doubt whatsoever that there was a very definite 'Belgrano connection' between a seventy-eight-year-old Shropshire rose grower and that highly controversial episode in the Falklands War, even if it only existed in the paranoid minds of the security services and those who authorised the search for leaks.

SIX

The Matter Before the House

To MENTION briefly my own part in this, after I had been persuaded that there was something very odd about the death of Hilda Murrell which was worth looking into, I began to get together material for a feature piece. As a free lance without any kind of back-up, either financial our journalistic, it was extremely difficult to try to piece together such a complex story. My first efforts to place it with the newspaper for which I have worked and to which I have contributed for over twenty years failed dismally. It was felt that the handling of the piece raised too many difficulties.

Determined to get it out into the open one way or another I then went to the *New Statesman*, to which I have also contributed for many years. The editor, Hugh Stephenson, gave the go-ahead, after mutual agreement that more work needed to be done, and handed the project over to the *New Statesman*'s deputy editor, Sarah Benton.

Rob Green had been certain from the outset that his aunt's death was in some way connected with her work but had decided not to do anything which would in any way detract from the paper he was to read on her behalf at Sizewell, until after that event took place. He read the paper on September 13th at The Maltings, Snape.

He had been far from satisfied with the way the police had handled the enquiry and with the string of discrepancies, from the 'ransacked' house and the 'sexual assault' to the long delay over tracing the ownership of the car. He felt that, at the very best, the way the police had handled the enquiries in the early stages was inept and he did a good deal of research into the matter on his own. This had led to the statement by Mr Gerard Morgan-Grenville about the strange and worrying remark made to him by Hilda Murrell in the February, which Mr Morgan-Grenville also told to the police, and to the discovery that Mr Scott had not seen a body in the copse on the Thursday after she was killed. Altogether, he found the series of police dissimulations and the contradictory information they gave to him a cause for acute concern.

After very lengthy discussions with Rob Green a draft piece was submitted to the *New Statesman* obviously too full of detail to publish at length – there is simply insufficient space to run five- or six-thousand-word articles which is what would have been required to include all the detail collected by that time. It was a matter of deciding what could be left out, how to make a coherent but brief narrative of such a difficult story, and what could safely be said without either breaking the law or provoking a libel action.

I was fully aware of the '*Belgrano* connection' but I had promised Rob Green that I would not make an issue of this. Apart from anything else, I felt strongly that it could put him at risk, at best, of being charged under section 2 of the 1911 Official Secrets Act on the assumption that he had passed on information, which he had not, or, at worst, putting him and his wife, Liz, at personal risk from the people who had decided that they wanted to know what Hilda Murrell was up to.

The form of words finally settled on was that he played 'a crucial role in the Falklands War' and it was mentioned that he had received a citation for services to this country. This would almost certainly have been enough to interest Tam Dalyell but he says that on the day before the piece went into the *New Statesman* (November 9th, 1984) he received an anonymous telephone call drawing his attention to the next issue and asking him to read the piece carefully, which he did.

Over the next weeks we corresponded and exchanged limited information in guarded telephone calls. Both of us have worked on the assumption that our telephone lines are tapped. I had it on extremely good authority, by somebody who should know, that mine was tapped while I was living and working in the Midlands before moving to my present address.

Dalyell himself, who has many connections in high places as the last chapter showed, now began to make enquiries on his own account. He, unlike many people including myself, discounts the theory that the nuclear issue had anything to do with the break-in, but this is irrelevant to what he was to discover.

There is no reason to disbelieve him, on past form, when he says he has sources on intelligence operations which are both extremely reliable and authoritative. He says that the reason the particular source who gave him information on Hilda Murrell had not come forward before was because of the extreme concern felt throughout the civil service owing to the coming trial of Clive Ponting. Ponting's colleagues did not want to stand beside him in the dock.

Dalyell's understanding of what happened, according to his sources, is this. The operation was not organised at a high level initially. There had been no intention whatsoever of harming Hilda Murrell (something on which everybody is agreed). It had been decided to make a search of her house to see if she had any copies of documents and raw signals to do with the sinking of the *Belgrano* that incriminated the government, some of which had been destroyed on instructions at a very high level by the intelligence services. On March 21st, two intruders, not one, went into her house while she was out. She came back and unexpectedly disturbed them and there was a struggle in which she was severely injured. She was then taken away and either killed or left to die of hypothermia and the cover up had to begin, because the searchers were men of the British Intelligence.

Throughout the whole affair there has been no contact between Tam Dalyell and Rob Green although Rob Green has been in close touch with his own MP, Paddy Ashdown, Liberal MP for Yeovil.

On December 18th, Tam Dalyell learned he had drawn a high place in the 'lottery' for speakers in the Consolidated Fund debate. This is the 'end of term' event in the House of Commons which enables a few lucky MPs to raise any matter which they think to be of sufficient concern to the House. It gave Dalyell, therefore, the opportunity for which he had been waiting to make a full statement on the death of Hilda Murrell. On the eve of the debate which began on December 19th and went on into the early hours of December 20th, he rang me with the statement he was going to make giving me information that up until then I had been totally unaware of, most especially that two intruders had been involved, not one. At the same time Paddy Ashdown contacted Rob Green to read out to him over the telephone Dalyell's very lengthy statement in order to get his comments upon it.

At 3.51 a.m. precisely, in the early hours of December 20th, Dalyell rose and addressed a tired and sleepy House. He began by explaining how his interest had been aroused by the report of Hilda Murrell's death in the *New Statesman* and he gave MPs the bare bones of the murder, pointing out that the inquest had produced a verdict of 'unlawful killing'.

Approaching one of his numerous sources on the *Belgrano*

. . . who has proved careful, accurate and serious, I learnt that Miss Murrell's nephew Rob Green, mentioned in the article by name, had indeed occupied a key position in naval intelligence during the Falklands campaign. I was informed that Commander Green was in a position to know about the receipt and dispatch of signals to and from HMS *Conqueror*, and intercepted signals from the *Belgrano* to the Argentine mainland and back, from both British and American sources.

He emphasised that he had had no personal contact with Rob Green who, to the 'best of my extensive knowledge . . . has behaved absolutely properly as a naval officer loyal to the navy in not talking about information gleaned when in the navy'.

Dalyell then took the House through the many discrepancies and anomalies in the Hilda Murrell story – the prolonged wait for the tracing of the car number, the 'ransacking', and so on.

Does a police force which, I am told, has a good reputation for efficiency, normally act like that or was it told on high authority to act in such an uncharacteristic and slap-dash way? Why did the police behave out of character? Ministers should tell us. I am told by more than one of the people interviewed by the police that they instinctively felt that the police officers knew jolly well that their time was being wasted and that they were having to go through the motions of a large scale investigation for cosmetic reasons.

Dalyell himself had nothing but praise for the behaviour of the local police in general. Having mentioned that the Special Branch had also been brought in on the case he said:

I can easily understand the work of the local police under Chief Detective Superintendent David Cole, brought in from Worcester, whose manners appear to have been exemplary and whose kindness and good sense is a credit to the police of this country. However, the local police have, I gather, now agreed that the Special Branch was involved and I understand that my praise for the local police does not in all cases apply to the Special Branch. Will the Minister explain what Special Branch was doing so early in the case of a murder of a seventy-eight-year-old rose grower, if it really was a simple burglary?

He then went on to ask why the family had been refused details of both autopsy reports. 'Did she, as the police say, die of hypothermia? Or was she killed by a person or persons?' He also asked why the cremation was carried out 'in a heck of an indecent hurry', and 'why were the family not told they could have an independent autopsy?' Why, indeed. It was Ron Smith's insistence on getting in an outside and totally independent Danish pathologist to carry out an autopsy on his behalf on the body of his daughter, Helen, which showed not only that a good deal of information given to him about the previous post mortems was incomplete but that it was extremely doubtful that she could have fallen from the height claimed. It also showed she had been the victim of a brutal sexual assault. An independent autopsy would, at least, have given the Greens something to hold on to after Hilda Murrell's body had been cremated.

He drew attention to Scott's statement that there was no body to be seen in the copse on the Thursday afternoon of March 22nd adding, 'I understand that a local poacher has now come forward to corroborate Mr Scott's statement that there was no body in that copse on the Thursday afternoon.'

He quoted Hilda Murrell's statement to Gerard Morgan-Grenville and then turned his attention to the nuclear connection. Dalyell has always been a supporter of nuclear power and has many friends at the highest level within the industry. He stated firmly that he was sure that nobody within that industry 'would dream of authorising minions to search the house of a seventy-eight-year-old rose grower who had elegantly expressed, but unoriginal, views on reactor choice and nuclear waste disposal . . . those people would not fuss about Hilda Murrell and her evidence, for heaven's sake'.

He then quoted Rob Green saying 'I am led to one solution only – that the break-in was to look for information, rather than valuables.'

He further quotes Rob Green:

I have a series of questions I want to ask about the police handling of the case, particularly their view of the proposition that the intruder – because he had no authority to kill her – had no alternative but to abduct her. Later that night he may have returned, put on the lights and drawn the curtains to make it look like an attempted burglary. He also left evidence [the handkerchief with semen stains] to suggest a sex angle.

The inquest, he said, raised more real questions than it answered.

Dalyell then explained why he had brought the matter before the full House and not gone privately to Home Secretary, Leon Brittan.

I must candidly tell the Minister that in my previous twenty-two years in the House, I should have gone privately to the Home Secretary, regardless of party. I should have gone to 'Rab' Butler, Henry Brooke, Frank Soskice, the Rt Hon. Member for Glasgow Hillhead (Roy Jenkins), my Rt Hon. friend for Cardiff South and Penarth (Jim Callaghan), my Rt Hon. friend for Morley and Leeds South (Merlyn Rees) or to Willie Whitelaw. I have known them all and had dealings with all of them. However, to some ministers in the present government, to whom I have been the subject of ridicule and deception, I am not prepared to go . . . least of all am I prepared to go to the present Home Secretary, who makes the type of speech about the miners that brings disgrace to the great office that he holds. I am simply not prepared to go to the present home secretary.

The story that I am told is as follows. In the early spring, the Prime Minister and ministers close to her were getting very nervy about incessant questioning about the *Belgrano* in general and about signals, intercepted signals and GCHQ at Cheltenham, which would call into question their truthfulness to the House in particular. This was pre-Ponting. There were a number of suspicions about people, dating from December 19th and 20th, 1983, when I tabled questions to the Prime Minister about GCHQ Cheltenham which are recorded on the Order Paper and Hansard.

Because Commander Robert Green was known to be unhappy about certain aspects of the Falklands War and was known to have wanted to leave the navy, he came under a cloud of suspicion, wrongly to the best of my knowledge, but certainly under a cloud . . . it was thought he might have copies of documents and raw signals, some of the originals of which had been destroyed by the intelligence services.

Just as those of us who have had certain documents have taken the precaution of keeping them in friends' or relatives' houses while we have them, so it was thought that some of Rob Green's supposed records might be in the home of the aunt to whom he was close.

Green, he said, was one of the very few men who left the navy about that time although he had decided to go before the war started.

I am also given to understand – and I am happy to accept it – that there was no premeditated intention of doing away with Miss Murrell – only a search of her house when she was out. Alas, on Wednesday March 21st she returned unexpectedly to change. The intruders either

arrived while she was dressing or were disturbed by her.
Being a lady of courage and spunk, often found in that
generation of women, Miss Murrell fought them. They
too had to fight. They injured her and panicked.

I am informed that the intruders were not after money
or nuclear information, but were checking the house to
see if there were any *Belgrano*-related documents of
Commander Green in the home of his aunt. Things went
disastrously wrong. They had no intention of injuring,
let alone killing, a seventy-eight-year-old ex rose grower.
Yet, being the lady she was and in her home, Hilda
Murrell fought and was severely injured. She was then
killed or left to die from hypothermia, and the cover up
had to begin because I am informed the searchers were
men of the British Intelligence.

If ministers cannot solemnly deny my belief about
the participation of intelligence, on whose ministerial
authority, if any, did the search of Miss Murrell's home
take place? Was there clearance, or was this the intelligence service 'doing their own thing'? Did they do it on
political orders, and if so, on whose orders? Some of us
have had increasing misgivings about the role of the
intelligences services in this country – in connection with
the miners' strike.

He concluded that it was high time there was a Select
Committee of Privy Councillors, 'to keep an eye on our
intelligence services'. Such a Select Committee would be a
more appropriate forum than a Consolidated Fund debate,
'but until that happens and given my opinion of present
senior ministers – unBritish in their behaviour compared
with ministers of previous governments – I have no alternative but to ask these questions under the cloak of Parliamentary privilege, none of the situations for which the
privileges of the House of Commons exist'.

He was supported by Paddy Ashdown who described
Dalyell as a man who 'performs a great service by introduc-

ing deeply and carefully researched questions of this kind'. Rob Green, he said, was a member of the Liberal Association in his own constituency and he had known for some time about the death of Miss Murrell. But the details given by Dalyell, as to the manner of it, had only been told him the previous evening when Dalyell had shown him what he was intending to say.

Faced with Dalyell's proposed statement to the House, Paddy Ashdown had rung Rob Green and read it over to him. 'I have his authority to say that he corroborated all that the hon. member has said. The details and facts are precisely as Commander Green sees them. Where the hon. member has referred to Commander Green, Commander Green assures me that he agreed with the hon. member's references.'

He emphasised that Rob Green had also corroborated that he at no time had been in touch in any way with Tam Dalyell but as he agreed with what had been said, Dalyell had 'not taken the name of Commander Green in vain'.

Pointing out that all too many of Dalyell's questions had been greeted with 'ridicule' in the past, only to have proved later to be all too well founded, he hoped that all Dalyell's questions would be answered in a proper manner by the Minister but if there were no detailed and acceptable answers to the detailed questions then he felt the only way forward would be 'to call for a full inquiry in front of a High Court judge'.

He pointed out that many of the government's actions following the *Belgrano* incident had led even those who would like to support it in the difficult decisions that had to be taken in time of war to be suspicious, and the government's campaign of misinformation and inadequate answers to questions has kept the *Belgrano* issue alive and caused concern among those who would like to be able to support the actions taken regarding the cruiser.

He also supported Dalyell on the broader issue of the intelligence services, then launched into a passionate appeal for the intelligence services to be brought 'under appropriate political control. Indeed, I would go further and say that the intelligence services can do their job effectively only if they are closely connected with the whole political system, are very much under political control and are able to influence the political system in an appropriate and proper fashion.'

Then he came to the nub of his whole speech. 'At the very heart of this issue lies the system that we now refer to as "clearance". The intelligence services have to receive clearances before taking any action.'

He felt sure that there would have to be approval, under normal circumstances, for action such as that mentioned by Tam Dalyell.

If what the hon. member says is true, it is inconceivable that it could have occurred under normal circumstances . . . But if that did not happen, there must have been a significant breakdown in the way that our intelligence services are controlled . . . there must have been a very serious breakdown in the democratic and political accountability and control of our intelligence services.

Clive Soley, Labour MP for Hammersmith, then asked for 'in due course a satisfactory explanation of events' or the setting up of an enquiry even if the story as recounted 'would tax the ingenuity of a novelist'. He then continued, saying, 'not only is my hon. friend's research accurate, but so are the sources of his information. I know those to be extremely good sources of information. The Minister and many others must be deeply disturbed by the quality of the information that is always available to my hon. friend.'

He, too, called for stricter control of the intelligence services. 'The security forces have grown in number and sophistication in recent years and to rely on the control of either the Home Secretary or the Prime Minister, answerable to the House, must be grossly inadequate in any

democracy.' He questioned the need for a Select Committee of privy councillors saying that it was felt on the Labour
benches that a House Select Committee of MPs would do
the job responsibly and adequately.

He concluded by saying that we could not go on much
longer with the present system of control. It brought the
country into disrepute and left unanswered questions such
as those raised by Dalyell. It was a fundamentally dangerous situation for any democracy to find itself in and 'if the
public feel that there are cover ups and people trying
to avoid difficult questions and that the structure of the
democracy is not good enough to bring matters out, the
credibility of that democracy will be undermined'.

At 4.33 a.m. Giles Shaw, Minister of State for the Home
Office rose to reply. Mr Shaw is a reasonable man and
every sympathy should be extended to him in the situation
in which he found himself. He had not been aware of the
implications of the matter which was to be put before the
House. He therefore apologised for being unable to answer
the questions adequately in the circumstances and to any
'lack of courtesy' because of this. The inferences drawn,
he said, went substantially beyond the matter sent down
for debate and went on to include a different form of
control of the nation's security services. With regard to the
police enquiry, had the assailant been caught then many
of the questions may well have been answered.

He had made some enquiries into the case following an
earlier attempt by Dalyell to raise the matter in the House
and he had received certain information from the chief
constable of West Mercia . . . 'I must draw attention – as
I believe I have – to the fact that the story is incomplete.
There are some facts which it would be inappropriate for
me to disclose. If I did so, it might hinder the police
enquiries that are continuing and might prejudice their
questioning of any suspect who might be apprehended.'

He then detailed the events of the week of Hilda Murrell's death from the viewpoint of the police – omitting,

however, any mention of ransacked houses or sexual assaults. It would seem that even the result of the inquest *still* left the cause of death uncertain, as the Minister says that she was beaten, stabbed 'and, possibly, as the coroner subsequently concluded, left to die of hypothermia'. Police who turned up to investigate her car 'within an hour' of its first being reported on the Wednesday afternoon found 'no suspicious circumstances' and treated it as an abandoned vehicle. After discovering on the Friday to whom the car belonged (following the second reporting of it) a constable had called at the house early in the evening and although he found the back door unlocked, assumed nothing was amiss and did not search the house 'despite being unable to make contact with anybody there'.

Since the finding of the body police enquiries had been extensive. Over a hundred people were identified as being in the area of Sutton Road on the days preceding her murder, over fifty on the actual day. Tracing these people formed a major part of the police enquiry.

Substantial resources had been devoted to trying to find Miss Murrell's killer. Some 3,500 men had been suggested as the potential offender by the public, police officers or by research on local and national intelligence indexes. Out of this number, 962 people have been identified for interview, and over half of them have already been interviewed. Over 1,300 telephone messages had been received by November 30th, over 2,000 statements taken and over 55,000 items of information recorded, both manually and on computer in the incident room.

As at November 30th, nearly 12,000 people had been interviewed, over 4,500 houses visited and over 1,500 vehicles checked. This gave some idea of the tenacity and thoroughness of the police investigation. There had been a 'massive orthodox investigation' into the tragic events surrounding Miss Murrell's death.

Early in the investigation the police had taken Miss Murrell's nuclear activities into account, and Shaw expressed himself as grateful to Dalyell 'for dismissing the suggestion out of hand' that the nuclear power lobby could have been in any way involved. West Mercia police had sought the assistance of other forces 'here and overseas' to prepare a profile of the likely offender, and the profile delivered to them by these other forces had 'closely mirrored' the picture formed by the West Mercia police themselves. The inquest on December 5th had brought in a verdict of 'unlawful killing' and decided that Miss Murrell died 'probably' on March 21st as a result of hypothermia.

As to the questions on the involvement of the security services, these went beyond the remit of the Home Office and would receive 'a proper considered response'. He would give an undertaking to that effect.

Tam thanked the Minister for the seriousness of his reply and said he would be prepared to wait – weeks if necessary – for proper answers to his questions. Mr Shaw noted that. 'I take note that the hon. gentleman has expressed substantial criticism of the reputation of the Home Office. I regret that fact, but I assure the hon. gentleman that the debate and the questions will obtain full consideration and a proper and comprehensive reply in the manner wished by the hon. gentleman, myself, and, no doubt the House.'

The Minister sat down. It was 4.53 a.m. and the House then went on to debate a motion by Mr Robert B. Jones, MP for Hertfordshire West, on the financing of the BBC. As he rightly put it, 'Shortly before five o'clock in the morning is perhaps not the happiest time to consider such an important subject.'

SEVEN

Under Surveillance

BEFORE COMING to the furore which Tam Dalyell's questions in the House was to raise, just who did he mean by 'men from British Intelligence', and who might be involved in such surveillance activity? There is, in fact, a rather wide choice and much overlapping.

Why should Hilda Murrell have been on anybody's file – why should any of us? Well, according to a detailed report in the *Guardian* on April 18th, 1984 some 500,000 of us have our names stored on file on the first floor of MI5 headquarters in London alone. The folders contain documents, photographs and typed records of our beliefs, activities, friends, families, jobs and homes and any allegations of suspicions about us. That's an awful lot of people considered as worthy of surveillance.

Members of CND and other anti nuclear protestors have long been in the category of those considered fair game for MI5 and the Special Branch, of which more later. In fact the sheer numbers of those who now come within the scope of our security services mean that either we have the biggest proportion of subversives in the world or the whole system has got out of control.

A whole section of MI5, known as F branch is devoted solely to what is termed 'domestic subversion'. Among 'targets' which have been monitored by F division and/or the Special Branch are the Woodcraft Folk (the children's section of the Co-operative movement), the hunt saboteurs, the organisers of a ball at Keele University to which royalty was expected and an entire class studying Marxism and Literature at Gwent College of Further Education (*Guardian*, April 19th, 1984). Tough stuff.

Regional officers of MI5 provide a direct link between MI5 and each local Special Branch. On August 17th, 1984, after Hilda Murrell's death but before the story broke, Duncan Campbell, writing in the *New Statesman* discussed the purpose and activities of MI5's A (Operations) branch. Until then this information was so secret it had not even been revealed to Cabinet and Home Office officials supposed to supervise the internal activities of MI5. 'The purpose of this secrecy', writes Campbell, 'is to enable ministers and orthodox civil servants to continue to deny any knowledge that MI5 breaks the law as it applies to others, with impunity.'

Under this control comes the AIA branch which is responsible for collecting improperly gathered information, which transcribes legal and illegal telephone taps and organises illegal break-ins.

MPs have complained many times to the Home Secretary about the apparent *carte blanche* this group has to break the law in any way that suits it which, writes Campbell, 'has frequently been demonstrated by break-ins, against political groups. Although members . . . have so far escaped public prosecution on the occasions the police have caught them at their work, it can only be a matter of time before an MI5 burglary goes wrong.' There is no proof that those who broke into Hilda Murrell's house were working for the AIA group, the 'specialists in official thefts and break-ins', but Campbell's words have a prophetic ring, coupled with 'a burglary that went tragically wrong'.

But most often the work of monitoring a 'soft' target (as Hilda Murrell would be described), would go to the Special Branch. Officially the Special Branch is not a national body, it is made up of officers from the different police forces under the control of the chief constables of each area. The Special Branch lards its activities with exotic names. 'Still life' is the name given to the collection of membership lists of organisations considered worthy of surveillance and it is quite likely that the Sizewell objectors came under this loose heading. This is considered, according to a source quoted in the *Guardian* (April 18th, 1984) as 'the most valuable single source on subversives'.

During hearings before the Commons' Home Affairs Committee in January 1985, the head of Scotland Yard's Special Branch told the Committee that its job was to 'help the security services defend the realm'. (*Guardian*, January 24th, 1985.) Deputy Assistant Commissioner Colin Hewett said that one aspect of the work carried out by the 400 members of Special Branch was assessing strengths of demonstrations. Records of possible subversives were kept on computer, not on file, but he denied that all Peace Movement supporters were automatically logged although he refused to say how many files were kept 'as it would be against the public interest'.

The chief constable of Northamptonshire, Mr Maurice Buck, said his force only employed seven Special Branch men out of 1,000 officers but that they held between 400 and 500 files. Mr Kenneth Oxford, chief constable of Merseyside said his Special Branch was made up of 178 officers out of 4,700 policemen and they kept 'several hundreds, probably thousands' of records. He also admitted that Special Branch information had sometimes leaked out to unauthorised people but that these rare occurrences were regretted. His computer, however, had fewer names on it now than two years ago.

If anybody thinks that Hilda Murrell with her anti Sizewell activities and her *Belgrano* connection was not sufficiently interesting to attract the attention of the Special Branch then one can only point to Mrs Madeleine Haigh who wrote a letter to the *Solihull News* a couple of years ago, expressing concern over the siting of Cruise missiles.

After repeated denials, she wrung from the then chief constable of the West Midlands police, Sir Philip Knight, an admission that she had been investigated by the Special Branch as a direct result of writing her letter. Commenting on it at the House of Commons Home Affairs Committee, Merseyside's Mr Kenneth Oxford said that possibly in her case the Special Branch had been 'over zealous'. He continued, 'There are a lot of over zealous police officers.'

When, for whatever reason, some kind of clandestine entry is required, most usually to look for documents, then very often MI5's AIA and the Special Branch combine on the operation. It would seem that the concern over such a burglary going wrong has not just been confined to those who dislike the whole idea of such activity but also to those who carry the operation out. They are told to proceed with great caution and are instucted not to steal anything even if this draws attention to the fact that while a house has been broken into and searched, nothing of real value has been taken away.

Again, according to the *Guardian* (April 18th, 1984), if something has to be stolen – like a document – then the Special Branch is used, as well as a policeman who takes an item away and can then claim he had a warrant (issued retrospectively) to search a house thus informing the local police force about what has gone on, before the irate owner of the property contacts them.

So now let us pass on to yet another secret police force. This is so secret that by contrast with it MI5's AIA and the Special Branch are open organisations with their information free to all. This is the special 'nuclear police'.

So secret are the nuclear police – and we do not even know how many there are of them, perhaps somewhere between 500 and 1000 – that they have their own chief constable whose annual report is classified as Top Secret. Everyone who joins the nuclear police has to be specially vetted by our old friends in MI5 and the Special Branch. Their full title is the United Kingdom Atomic Energy

Authority (UKAEA) Special Constabulary.

It really is one of life's ironies that this supersecret police force was given wide-ranging and almost unlimited extra powers by none other than that great champion of accountability and democracy, Tony Benn. Back in 1976, when he became Energy Minister, he gave them powers to carry a wide assortment of weapons, to travel well outside the areas immediately surrounding nuclear installations and had a clause put in the 1976 Special Constables Act which did all this saying a member could exercise his powers 'in any place where it appears to him expedient to go'. Naturally their prime function is to guard nuclear installations and nuclear waste on its way from the power stations to Sellafield but what else comes within their remit we do not know nor is it possible to find out. Mr Benn has since regretted his part in providing the extra powers.

There is no police committee to watch over the activities of the nuclear police; they are only accountable to the Atomic Energy Authority. In November 1983 in a BBC2 *Newsnight* inquiry into the nuclear police, reporter Gavin Essler said that many MPs were very concerned that this élite police force was simply the beginning of a growing security apparatus necessary to defend key civil nuclear sites as if they were top military secrets.

Ironically, in the same year that the nuclear police were being given their special powers, a warning came in the 1976 Report from the Royal Commission on environmental pollution, chaired by Lord Flowers, which said that it was 'highly likely and indeed inevitable' that a future nuclear security force would have to go on the offensive against terrorists or those who might be considered a danger to the nuclear industry. Their activities 'might include the use of informers, infiltrators, wire-tapping, checking on bank accounts and opening mail'.

It seems that even some chief constables are concerned about the possible extramural activities of the nuclear police who can cross boundaries between various police authorities with impunity. The chain of their command is that they are answerable to their own chief constable who is accountable to the board of the UKAEA. The board is answerable to the Energy Secretary who in theory is answerable to Parliament but in practice is not, as this is a topic which cannot be discussed by MPs.

Given that the possibility of a terrorist attack on a nuclear installation or on a flask of 'waste' is both a real and a horrific one, it is also a measure of the dilemma which faces the security services in a supposedly democratic society, that is, how far security must take precedence over civil liberties. It is not helped by the fact that the whole operation is shrouded in such secrecy from even those who are supposed to guard our rights.

Once again it is possible to quote a prophetic remark. Liberal MP Alan Beith who has persistently questioned and criticised the way in which the nuclear police are organised said, on the 1983 *Newsnight* programme that such police are in a privileged and potentially dangerous position. 'Sooner or later there is bound to be some sort of problem or mishap or misjudgement.'

AIA, the Special Branch and the nuclear police are 'official' operators of surveillance techniques. But, both MI5 and the Special Branch also regularly use outside infiltrators and informers to obtain information. We do not know under what circumstances this assistance is brought in.

On January 27th, 1985 Nick Davies, writing in the *Observer* revealed that objectors to the Sizewell enquiry had been the target of surveillance by a private detective agency with links with British Intelligence. This included all objectors – organisations such as the East Anglia Nuclear Alliance, environmental groups like Greenpeace and Friends of the Earth, and single objectors, presumably like Hilda Murrell. Names, addresses, telephone numbers, political leanings and any media links were gathered by private detectives. There is no suggestion that any of the independent security consultants which are affiliated to the Associate of Private Investigators have anything to do with Hilda Murrell's abduction. But the fact that there may be lone agencies, and that these have monitored the Sizewell objectors, is itself disturbing.

Private detectives were employed to infiltrate, to set up dummy peace groups and to monitor any objector of particular interest. The paper stressed that there was no reason to believe that this particular operation had been involved in the mystery surrounding the break-in at Hilda Murrell's house, but pointed out that the police seemed to be unaware that such an operation was taking place at all.

Documents obtained by the *Observer* state that the job of such agencies 'to provide security services of all kinds to government and other authorities', the work that the Home Office did not want their own operatives involved in. The director of one of these private agencies confided that he had been employed in January 1983 to monitor the objectors. He passed on the work with the brief: 'Client wishes to ascertain identities of principal objectors at the Sizewell atomic power enquiry at Snape Maltings. If possible, obtain list of objectors, their connections with the media, political leanings, etc.,' to other investigators.

It seems these people enthusiastically set about their task of finding out subversive groups and objectors although one wonders why they went to the trouble of undercover work to get lists of names and addresses of objectors as these are freely available at the enquiry office at Snape. This Inspector Clouseau-type activity would just be good for a laugh if the search had not widened to cover financial information about groups and to look into trade union and Labour Party members, and other possible objectors. It was also said that they had set up three 'dummy' peace groups which had been accepted by genuine peace group members and objectors and that they would be a useful tool to discredit, for example, CND.

It was emphasised again that this work had been under-

taken for a private client and although it was said initially
that the investigation had been mounted to seek out subversives, it was later claimed that the investigation had
'nothing to do with Whitehall'.

It was suggested that the client was a foreign company
anxious to find out the strength of opposition to the PWR
in Britain although this seems most odd and one wonders
what use a foreign company could have for such detailed
information about individual objectors. The police having
ruled out Hilda Murrell's Sizewell connection as having
had anything to do with her death, continue in this belief.
A spokesman for the CEGB was quoted in the *Guardian*
the next day as saying, 'We are not the clients and we
would in no way be involved in that sort of practice and
indeed we could not see what use the information would
be. It's evidence that matters and has done all the way
through, no matter what the antecedents of individuals
might be.'

There is – and it must be said again – no proof that any
of these organisations or a permutation of any of them
were involved in the death of Hilda Murrell apart from the
assertion of Tam Dalyell's source that British Intelligence
officers made the break-in.

In his *New Statesman* piece on August 17th, Duncan
Campbell pointed out that Britain remains the only
Anglo-Saxon country which has not seen a major inquiry
into the illegal activity of its security services in the last
ten years.

In reply to a letter from Labour MP John Prescott on
January 29th, 1984, Home Secretary Leon Brittan said that
the Special Branch must not be prevented from 'looking
into the activities of those whose real aim is to harm our
democracy but who, for tactical or other reasons, choose
to keep . . . within the letter of the law'. John Cunningham
described this as 'a *carte blanche*'.

EIGHT

Theories

FOLLOWING TAM DALYELL's intervention, the story broke
with a vengeance and the newspaper boards on the morning of Thursday December 20th, 1984 carried statements
like 'MP Shocks House' and 'MP Claims Cover Up' while
the early editions of the *Standard* devoted the entire front
page to the story, complete with two-inch headline 'MP's
Amazing Murder Story'. The media had finally discovered
Hilda Murrell.

Whatever the accuracy of Dalyell's source, his raising
the matter in the House provoked the first real media
activity since Hilda Murrell's death the previous March.
Interest was shown by newspapers and television com-
panies from all over the globe and more information came
trickling in, some useful, some doubtful. More pieces of
the jigsaw will be looked at in the next chapter.

But one result of the exposure the case received was
that it produced a wide, and wild, crop of theories as to
what had actually happened. These ranged from sub-Le
Carré plots to the possible. Few people seemed to accept,
in spite of what the police had to say, that Hilda Murrell
was killed by a passing burglar.

Perhaps we should begin with the last of all to get on to
it, the *Sunday Times*. The paper despatched a team of five
– four reporters and a researcher – to look into the murder
mystery. Under the headline 'Who Killed Hilda Murrell?'
the paper ran a full page piece on January 6th, 1985.

They told the story again of the break-in, the abduction, the leaving of the body, the cutting off of the telephones both in Shrewsbury and in Wales. They praised Tam Dalyell for exonerating the nuclear industry from conniving at the burglary and quoted his statement that he did not believe 'for one mini second' that Sir Walter Marshall of the CEGB could have authorised anything of the sort. Going on they advanced their own theory as to what happened.

This is that Rob Green and his aunt were natural suspects in the *Belgrano* leak enquiry. It is likely, it is admitted, that they might have been investigated by the security services and even kept under surveillance. In the middle of all this it is just possible, think the team, that a real-life bungling and perverted burglar then broke into Miss Murrell's house coincidentally. This would pose a problem to the security services who would then have to cover up *his* tracks in order to cover up their own. The instance of the cut telephone wires apparently lends 'some support to this theory'. The wires might well have been cut in order, for example, to remove a listening device. This theory would put the blame for the break-in and Hilda Murrell's death on the man the police want to help them with their enquiries as revealed by the FBI – white, unskilled, a loner, a habitué of pubs and local – but the responsibility for thoughtfully covering up his traces on to the intelligence services. But the *Sunday Times* team does admit that there are many difficulties and quotes Detective Superintendent Barrie Mayne as having said: 'This doesn't follow the accepted pattern of burglaries; not in my experience as a policeman.'

On the whole, a good deal of credence was given to the feeling that one of the security services was indeed involved with Hilda Murrell's death, although opinion was divided as to whether the reason for the break-in was her anti nuclear activity, the links with the *Belgrano* affair or a mixture of both.

Another possible reconstruction was put forward in *Pri-*

vate Eye on January 11th, which attempted to explain why she might have been abducted and not just left for dead on the floor of her bedroom. This suggests that strong-minded and alert as she was, she had been aware for some time that she was under surveillance – that would certainly fit in with her telephone call of February 25th and the information given to the Campbells on March 12th. She connected the surveillance solely with her Sizewell paper. On the morning she was killed she returned and, after going unsuspectingly into her house, found a strange man or men going through her papers. Being the kind of person she was she would certainly have made an enormous fuss about this, have taken the story to the media and would certainly have recognised the intruder(s) again. This would not only severely embarrass the intruder, it would do worse for whoever authorised his visit. If there was a struggle during which Hilda Murrell was knocked unconscious, this still left the intruder(s) with a problem, for she could not be found injured or dead in her own home without questions being asked about her anti nuclear connections. Possibly it was decided to fake some kind of accident for her, maybe a car accident; then the intruder(s) would return and tidy up the house after removing anything they wanted to take away.

The author of the *Private Eye* theory suggests that this was why Hilda Murrell was taken away, that she came round and tried to force her abductor off the road, that it was she, and not he, who threw a trail of belongings out of the car. There are some reports that suggest that there were also signs of a struggle inside the car. Turning the car into the lane, the battle forced the car off the road and slewed it over a rock.

Possibly her body was then hidden in a ditch while the intruder(s) returned, cut off the telephone, produced the 'evidence' of the semen-stained handkerchief (to make it look like a kinky killer) and thoroughly searched the house. The intruder(s) then returned on the evening of the

following day and removed Hilda Murrell's body and put
it into the copse where it was found, grateful that – for
whatever reason – Shrewsbury police had not followed up
properly the report of the abandoned car. *Private Eye*
posits the nuclear police as possible suspects.

There are a number of possible theories which could be
stretched to fit the facts. One of the principal objections
to the professional security service operator is the fact that
the job seems to have been such a botch. Given, after
tapping her telephone, that whoever it was assumed she
would be out all day and that she then returned unexpectedly, and given that the author of the *Private Eye* theory
is correct in suggesting that she saw the intruder(s) and
would recognise him/them again, there does seem to be a
real touch of panic hanging over the whole business.

Before the revelations of the *Observer* on January 27th,
that private agencies were monitoring Sizewell objectors,
yet another theory was that a couple of rather more ama-
teur operators had gone into Hilda Murrell's house. If
the Home Office have, according to the *Observer*
article, employed an agency to do work in the past
which it does not want to touch itself, is it not possible that
they employ other such agencies, especially if the target is
a 'soft' one? There would be very definite advantages. It
could truthfully be denied, if such an operation went
wrong, that the official security services had been involved:
if the intruders were caught they could be treated as
ordinary burglars. But faced with the predicament in which
they found themselves, might not a couple of intruders
from some detective agency panic and make a mess of it
all? It would then be left to those who had directly employed them to try and cover up the traces and pick up the
pieces.

If anything further was needed to spell out the truth of
this secret world then Paul Foot's story in the *Daily Mirror*
on January 31st, 1985 crowned it. This concerned the Mr
'Vic Norris' to whom the task of snooping on the Sizewell

objectors had finally been passed. It transpired that the same Vic Norris had been convicted in 1979 at Hertford-shire Assizes on charges concerning six sex offences involv-ing his young daughters. Two of the charges were for procuring one of his daughters, who was under sixteen, to have sex with a third party.

For this, Mr 'Norris' went to prison for six years and was released in 1973. In 1976 he again faced court charges and was convicted of carrying an offensive weapon. Shortly afterwards he featured in newspaper stories as the leader of a satanist sect calling themselves the Anglian Satanic Church. He was also the founder of a group called the Nazi Phoenix Society and another organisation called the 5000 Group. The Sizewell job eventually came to Norris from a member of the Institute of Professional Investi-gators and who handed it out to another member of the institute, a Mr Barrie Peachman. However, Mr Peachman committed suicide last year but before doing so handed the Sizewell contract over to Vic Norris. Vic Norris also calls himself Adrian Hampson and runs a debt collection agency in Colchester.

As Paul Foot emphasises, nobody is saying that Mr Norris-or-Hampson, or anyone he employs, broke into Hilda Murrell's house but it is a chilling thought that such people can be employed to watch Sizewell objectors and even more disturbing that they can be acceptable to and used by the Home Office.

Certainly there have been cases in the past of the security services and Special Branch using such paid outside assist-ance. On the Easter Saturday of 1974 a thirty-year-old Irishman, Kenneth Joseph Lennon, was found dead in a ditch. He had been shot three times in the head by a .38 revolver. Almost immediately, the events preceding his death were revealed. Lennon had been a paid Special Branch agent and informer; he had also, earlier on, played a double game with the IRA. Three days before he was killed he had come to London to report to the Special

Branch officers to whom he was responsible, and whatever happened at that meeting put Lennon in fear of his life. He was so terrified that he approached, first of all, the jazz singer George Melly, telling him he was being pursued by both the IRA and Special Branch. When, not surprisingly, Melly seemed doubtful he went on to the National Council for Civil Liberties (NCCL) where he made a 'confession' of his Special Branch involvement in which he said that because of him men were serving long prison sentences and that he himself had got off a serious charge because his trial was rigged to secure his acquittal. Most of what he said later turned out to be true.

During those last two meetings he said two crucial things. To Melly he said: 'You think my story is fantasy. If you read in the papers I've been found face down in a puddle or a ditch, you'll know I've been speaking the truth.' To the NCCL he said: 'I shouldn't be surprised if the Special Branch did me in and made it look like an IRA job.'

A nationwide murder hunt has never revealed the slightest clue as to Lennon's killer or killers. An enquiry into the events leading up to his death did not push matters much further either, although it did confirm that he had indeed been involved in a phony acquittal.

In his book on the Lennon affair, *Reluctant Judas* (Temple Smith, 1976), barrister Geoffrey Robertson points out that the head of the security services has no duty to inform either the government or the home secretary as to all the operations it carries out.

There is something of Lennon's plight in both the death of Hilda Murrell, the victim, and the position in which her murderer now finds himself if he has been employed by the security services. Like Lennon, Hilda Murrell considered her life at risk and had told people so. Like Lennon, though, anybody employed by the security services who killed Hilda Murrell in the course of a robbery carried out on their orders would be in an almost impossible position – and the fate of Lennon came to mind more than once during my investigations into the Hilda Murrell affair. For what would there be to connect, say, the unexplained death in a ditch of a man in East Anglia, or in Devon, or Scotland with what happened to Hilda Murrell? It would just be another unexplained murder which even a nation-wide murder hunt would fail to solve.

When Tam Dalyell had first made the claim about Hilda Murrell's murder and the involvement of the security services in it, Giles Shaw had promised him that he would give it 'full consideration and a comprehensive reply', and Dalyell had responded, as we have seen, that he did not mind how long it took so long as it was done properly. However, nine days later Giles Shaw told Dalyell in a letter that: 'I am now able to state unreservedly that your allegations about the intelligence services being involved are totally without foundation.' This statement was made *before* the police were to undertake enquiries as to whether or not Tam Dalyell's statement might possibly be true . . .

Dalyell's reply to that was: 'This is just typical of the whole *Belgrano* saga: claims are dismissed before they have been properly considered and then, sooner or later, lo and behold! the claims turn out to be true. I think that Giles Shaw has simply gone through his officials to the security services and asked them, and they've said: "There's nothing in it, old boy."'

I was asked on the BBC's *The World at One* programme if I was 'disappointed' that Mr Shaw had replied in such a way. I could only say that I had hardly expected he would stand up in the House with his hand on his heart and say, 'Sorry, Tam old boy, one of our chaps went in there and got it wrong . . .' *The World at One*, by the by, after considerable enquiries on a story which they told me 'stood up' dropped the whole issue.

On January 17th in a more lengthy written reply, Giles Shaw replied in detail to some of the points Tam had raised. He confirmed that there was evidence within the house 'of a thorough and systematic search' and also of signs of a struggle. He understood from the chief constable that the term 'ransacked' was an exaggeration of the true extent of the disorder and 'had not been used by the police in describing the break-in'. The telephone wires, according to Mr shaw, were 'pulled out'. Certainly the police had said originally that the wires had been disconnected at the junction box but after 'subsequent checks' they had changed their minds and discovered, after all, that the wires had just been ripped out. The difficulty was that the screws could be loosened if the wires were removed from the junction box by force; the fact remains that the phone was cut off.

There was no sign of a sexual assault on the victim. There were, however, signs in the house of 'some attempted sexual activity' but for fear of distressing the family and for 'properly operational reasons' the chief constable was 'unable to disclose details of what these signs are'. This compares somewhat oddly with the *Shropshire Star* of April 19th, 1984, with its headline 'Sex Attack on Murdered Woman – Police' followed by '. . . the murdered woman was a victim of a sex attack, police revealed today. "This is a particularly disgusting thing, an assault of this nature on a seventy-eight-year-old woman," Detective Chief Superintendent David Cole said.' However, this evidence does fit in with the theory that the sexual aspect of the attack was simulated.

Two officers had examined her abandoned car 'within two hours of her death' but as there were no suspicious circumstances and no apparent danger or obstruction to the public from it, they took no further direct action. I was told the car number had been checked out on the Friday and not earlier as the police were too busy to follow up every abandoned car in an area where 2,000 were abandoned every year. Rob Green had been told that an incorrect number fed into the computer had led the police to a car owner in Scotland. Giles Shaw states a third version. The police checked the registration of the car number *immediately* and *immediately* obtained the correct name and address of the keeper. The chief constable denied that Rob Green had ever been told that the wrong registration number was fed into the computer, and there was no reference to the answer made to me on his behalf – that the car number had not been followed up until the Friday as the car had been treated as an abandoned vehicle.

Giles Shaw admits there were some discrepancies in his first statement of the sequence of events on the Friday evening and Saturday morning as first told to the House but says that attempts made to contact Miss Murrell later on the Friday night were by telephone and not by visit, although a police officer had called in and found the door unlocked and a light on earlier in the evening and a policeman called first at 7 a.m. and then again at 8.15 a.m. the following day.

The West Mercia Special Branch had been called in early in the investigation for a short while and that ended the involvement of that force's Special Branch but 'experienced detective officers from Special Branch were subsequently used, not in any respect in a Special Branch role, but to assist in routine work connected with this major murder enquiry which placed a very heavy burden on the detective manpower of a relatively small force'.

As to the refusal of the post mortem details to the family, this matter was entirely within the discretion of the coroner and was 'not one in which I would intervene'. The family's solicitor, says Mr Shaw, would have been expected to inform the family they were entitled to an independent autopsy, not the coroner nor the police. The death is recorded officially as hypothermia. The reason for the hasty request to remove the body was as stated to Rob Green and there was no substantiation of the opinion of Mr Ian Scott that there was no body in the copse on the Thursday afternoon. The Home Office pathologist had stated that the position of the body was consistent with it having lain there since the Wednesday afternoon. Apart from Mr and Mrs Morgan-Grenville, no other witnesses had said that Hilda Murrell had been concerned about her personal safety.

So there the matter rests. Or does it? Among the miscellaneous pieces of information which came in either to the media or the Greens was one rather remarkable item, in view of the constant reiteration that nothing except the fifty pounds had been taken from her house. For it seems that the unfinished version of her Sizewell paper, the only one found in her house, was *not* the only one that should have been there. It now appears that she had told at least two people, shortly before her death, that she had *finished* her Sizewell paper and the paper she described was not the unfinished and only version found in her home. So what happened to that? It is just another piece of the jigsaw to be looked at next, along with the sequence of events which followed the raising of the matter in the House of Commons on December 20th, 1984.

NINE

Pieces of a Jigsaw

IN THE wake of Dalyell's statement in the House, more information slowly began to come in, some interesting, some useful, some which was both and also, as is always the way with this kind of thing, some which was neither.

It seemed that two people at least had been suspected by the police, working on the burglar theory, of murdering Hilda Murrell. Robert James Higgins, awaiting sentence for a number of offences, told the press on January 8th, 1985 through his solicitor that he felt the police were trying to pin the murder on him.

Higgins had been picked out in an identity parade by a woman who thought he might have been the 'running man' seen on the road to Shrewsbury on the afternoon after Hilda's murder.

Higgins felt the circumstantial evidence against him was formidable. The police case rested on three main points. Firstly, he can drive but has never passed his test. He says that if he was to get into a car and try to drive it then he might well drive it 'erratically', as the witnesses who saw Hilda's car on the Wednesday morning described the manner in which it was being driven. Secondly, he admits that he did five burglaries in the area near to where Hilda Murrell lived. Thirdly, not only was he picked out by a witness, he is something of a runner and runs for exercise. He can manage up to fifteen miles without any problems at all. He admits to having run away from houses he has burgled and the police allege they found an entry in his diary saying he had run seven miles on the day of Hilda Murrell's murder – roughly the distance between her home and Hunkington.

Higgins pleaded guilty to two burglaries and a theft, asking for more than twenty other similar offences to be taken into consideration but he was very frightened indeed, he said. 'They were under pressure to find someone for that murder and I just didn't have an alibi. I couldn't remember where I was on the day. I didn't even know about the murder until they told me. At one stage I was desperate.'

Police had searched Higgins' flat in Birmingham where they found a pamphlet against nuclear weapons. Higgins states this was a coincidence. He might be a burglar but he is still interested in the nuclear issue. 'It's something I think everyone should be interested in. It affects us all and I think it's a good idea to know where you are.'

Higgins was taken by the police to Hilda Murrell's house. He swears he had never been there before in his life. 'I didn't recognise the place.'

Further nightmares were in store when he was then picked out from an identity parade. 'That's it,' I thought, 'they'll charge me.' He was closely questioned about his driving and admitted freely to the police that had he driven the car he would probably have done it very badly but he stressed he had never even seen Hilda's car, let alone driven it through Shrewsbury. 'I was never there.'

Higgins was remanded in custody for two months on charges of burglary. In January 1985 his solicitor asked the court not to impose a further sentence beyond a ninety-days suspended term Higgins already faced following a conviction in Oxford, but he was kept on remand for sentence at Shrewsbury Crown Court. His solicitor, Mr Delwyn Williams, who gave Higgins' story to the *Standard* told the magistrates at Shrewsbury that his client had been interrogated at length as part of the hunt for Hilda Murrell's killer. 'He has been through hell,' he said.

Higgins says he felt the police were determined to prove he was the murderer but they never charged him. He has been extremely frightened that, he says, he 'might be framed'. But Higgins was not alone.

Tam Dalyell was contacted, the day after Higgins' story was made public, by a person who lives in North London. This person has a sister whose boyfriend we will call Peter, and the informant and his wife were looking after the couple's child as the couple had run into difficulties. In July the couple were living in a boarding house in Ramsgate and it was there, one evening, that Peter was arrested and taken into custody but not charged. When he asked why this was being done to him he was told it was in connection with the murder of Hilda Murrell.

He was first interrogated at length at Ramsgate and then taken to be questioned further at Shrewsbury. Shrewsbury CID told him they had heard a rumour he had been in Shrewsbury on the day that Hilda was murdered. Peter had indeed once lived in Shrewsbury but had left long before the murder. Not content with this, the police searched the home of Tam Dalyell's informant thoroughly, taking away various items and borrowing an affidavit to which, he says, they had no right. Peter and his girlfriend had actually been staying with the informant and his wife at the time of the Murrell murder but in spite of the informant's insistence that this was the case and that he could not possibly have been in Shrewsbury on that day, the police continued following up every possible lead in a search which took them first to Norwich, then to Dorset and finally back to London.

Peter has a long record of petty crime. The police emphasised throughout their interrogation that this was a murder hunt. Peter did not deny his petty criminal record. He was finally released three days later during which time he had confessed to a small burglary. He was never given access to a solicitor and when the informant queried this the police told him, 'He did not want one.'

Tam's informant was very worried indeed that Peter might have found himself charged with Hilda Murrell's murder, not least because the police had told him he closely resembled an identikit picture they had of the wanted man. (They did not say which picture.) When the informant asked the police if he could see the picture they said they had not remembered to bring it with them. Peter could not possibly have done it as he was in London at the time.

The police, as we have seen, have – they say – long discounted the theory that the murder might have had anything to do with Hilda Murrell's anti nuclear activities. Yet it appears they made extensive enquiries as to her connections, beginning in the April after her death and continuing at least into October 1984.

On April 3rd, 1984 a man living in Bedfordshire was contacted by the sub manager of his bank who said he had just received a telephone call from the police 'at the murder enquiry at Shrewsbury', in connection with the death of Hilda Murrell who had made annual payments of ten pounds by bankers order to the Nuclear Weapons Freeze Advertising Campaign, of which the man is secretary. The bank manager said that the police wished to speak to him, and was it all right if he gave the man's telephone number to them.

This was the first the secretary of NWFAC had heard of Hilda Murrell's death but he agreed and shortly afterwards received a call from a Detective Constable (name unknown) at Shrewsbury. He told the secretary that the police were trying to contact all the organisations with which she had connections and noted that among the organisations she supported was the NWFAC. Could he ask a few questions?

He asked how well the secretary had known Hilda Murrell, had he met her and whether he had had any recent contact with her. The secretary said that he had only known her by exchange of letters (although they had been in touch for twenty years), had never met her and had had no immediate recent contact with her.

On July 17th he was again telephoned from Shrewsbury, this time by 'Detective Constable Peters' with a question about a payment by Hilda Murrell of fifteen pounds to New Perspective Publishers Ltd. Could he tell him who and where they were? He could not.

The secretary of NWFAC was not alone in this. On October 18th, 1984, after West Mercia police had told me that they had discounted any anti nuclear connections with Hilda Murrell's death, Detective Chief Superintendent David Cole contacted Greenham Women Against Cruise. He wrote to them care of their bank account address in Highbury, London, saying that he was enquiring into the death of Hilda Murrell. It would appear, he said, that she had made a payment of thirty pounds by cheque to a Dr Lynne Jones 'who I believe is a member of the Greenham peace movement'.

'Would you confirm Dr Lynne Jones is a member of your movement, and if so, would she be good enough to contact the murder incident room at Shrewsbury police station to confirm receipt of the money from Miss Murrell and also to ascertain if Dr Jones has ever visited Miss Murrell at her home in Sutton Road, Shrewsbury.' Dr Jones had not visited Miss Murrell at her home. Like the secretary of NWFAC, she and Miss Murrell had merely exchanged letters.

It was after the statement in the House that Ian and Thalia Campbell contacted Tam Dalyell with the news that they had been told on March 12th that Hilda Murrell had fears for her personal safety. They were appalled when they learned of her death on the local news at twelve o'clock on March 24th, and Thalia Campbell telephoned Shrewsbury police to find out what had happened. The police told her they were looking for an intruder as the house had been 'ransacked' and turned over, and that it had obviously been a 'casual robbery'.

Later, they contacted the police again mentioning their concern over Hilda Murrell's anti nuclear activities and even going so far as to suggest that security services might have been involved. Thalia Campbell was telephoned back by an unnamed policeman of Shewsbury police asking what the Campbells' connection was with Hilda Murrell and if there had been any communication between them before she died. Ian Campbell says he tried, unsuccessfully, to interest the media in the case.

Campbell says the points that strike him are that Hilda Murrell was certainly worried about her safety some time before her death, that the police had specifically told them the house was 'ransacked' and that it was in such disorder that they were sure it must be a casual intruder, that this is now known not to be true and therefore 'either the police were incompetent or they were unprepared and did not all tell the same tale'. They felt, they said, concerned about their own safety in view of what had happened to Hilda Murrell.

On January 10th, 1985 the Home Office pathologist who carried out the first autopsy wrote a strong and somewhat pompous letter to *The Times*. Dr Acland has no doubts on the Hilda Murrell case at all but the speculation as to the mystery surrounding her death

. . . appears now to cast suspicion on the validity of the post mortem reports as well as the other allegations of impropriety in the police investigations.

Although I receive a retainer from the Home Office, I am jealous of my independence as a pathologist and I consider myself answerable only to Her Majesty's Coroner and the judiciary.

With respect to my involvement in the case, I carried out the post mortem examination to the best of my ability. I was given every assistance by the police (unlike

those who under the Coroner's Rules should have had
the report as 'properly interested persons') and was not
denied any information which I deemed relevant to help
me in my inquiries. I was not approached or influenced
by any member of the Secret Service organisation. I was
not aware of any involvement by such persons in the
case. I do not believe either that any of the involved
police officers were so influenced.

Dr Acland explained, again, why there had been a need
for a second post mortem so that a 'potential defendant'
could have the benefit of a second opinion 'so that the body
could be released for appropriate funeral arrangements. In
fact, the second pathologist kindly notified me that he
agreed with all my findings and conclusions.' He would, he
said, be happy to discuss his findings with any pathologist
nominated by the family.

'I don't know who killed Miss Murrell,' he concluded,
'but I have a strong suspicion that some twopenny-
halfpenny thief is gloating over a pint of beer in a pub not
many miles from Shrewsbury about all this media interest.'

If he is, then one can only wonder why the police have
not caught him.

On January 16th, 1985 came yet another piece of news.
A flat belonging to a Mr Peter Hurst, who worked with
Rob Green at naval headquarters during the Falklands
War, had been burgled on the night before Dalyell made
his statement to the House. Peter Hurst was the only other
naval officer, apart from Rob Green, who had left the
service since the Falklands War apart from those due for
retirement. His flat, which is in the middle of a block in St
Albans, was the only one broken into and although he
owns two television sets, a hi-fi and some small valuables,
nothing at all was taken. However, his papers had obviously been gone through.

As he told the *Daily Mirror* on January 16th, 1985 he
had at first thought it was an ordinary burglar. 'But now I

agree that it could just have some connection with the Hilda Murrell affair.' The police, however, discount any connections, going so far as to say even before their investigations are completed that they are sure the burglary has nothing to do with Hilda Murrell's murder. There have been several other burglaries in that part of St Albans . . .

On February 7th the *Standard* came out with some more information about the disconnection of Hilda Murrell's telephone. Whether or not the source inside British Telecom who revealed the information was the same one I spoke to at the beginning of January, I do not know, but it certainly confirmed my earlier information and, indeed, added to it.

The junction box had been removed in the way that I have already described and the green wire cut. This would certainly mean that those dialling would apparently hear the telephone ringing but the sound heard by the caller would occur at the exchange for the green lead governs the bell on the individual telephone set. Further, the scene-of-crime video, shown on BBC1's *Crimewatch* programme of March 14th, 1985 only shows wires lying freed from their socket. It does not reveal *how* the wires were disconnected. The *Standard* reporter went further. All telephones have a house card on file with British Telecom to record maintenance carried out, but the card for Hilda Murrell's number on file at the British Telecom depot at Ditherington, Shrewsbury, carries no reference either to the damage caused by the burglary or the subsequent investigation of that phone. In fact although the *Standard* did not say so, it is known that if a telephone is tapped then any faults arising on that telephone are kept on a separate card from the routine one and faults are repaired by special engineers involved in telephone tapping, not by routine engineers.

According to the engineer who leaked the information

to the *Standard* the details of what was found at Hilda Murrell's house with regard to the telephone are contained in a four-page hand-written report which was actually submitted to the police.

It appears that at one stage of the murder enquiry, a British Telecom engineer was intensively questioned by the police who believed his personal characteristics and technical knowledge made him a prime suspect.

While my own informant told me that the telephone in Hilda Murrell's Welsh holiday home had been disconnected in a similar way to that in her Shrewsbury house, the *Standard* report says that the police stated the telephone was out of order due 'to a capacitor fault caused by storm damage'. Yet friends of Hilda Murrell say her telephone was working right up to the time of her death and the *Standard*'s source says the only way the damage described by the police could have occurred would have been if the telephone line had been struck by lightning. He says that no lightning that could have caused such damage occurred in that area in either February or March of 1984. It is a strange coincidence then, if both telephones were out of order at the same time. It suggests much more than mere accidents.

So what do the police think of all this? Following Dalyell's questions the chief constable of West Mercia issued a statement saying that he would be talking to Tam Dalyell to find out if he could help them with their enquiries. He also confirmed that the Special Branch had been called in 'on a routine basis' because of manpower shortages and he further claimed that Dalyell's intervention and the media interests were 'hindering' the West Mercia police with their enquiries.

As to this latter point Hilda Murrell was murdered on March 21st, 1984 and her body found on March 24th. My own piece speculating that there might be something odd about her death went into the *New Statesman* on November 9th, 1984 – eight months afterwards. Tam Dalyell's intervention was a month after that, nine months after Hilda Murrell's death. One wonders, therefore, how such an intervention after so long a time could possibly hinder a murder enquiry which had been getting nowhere for months.

The police met Tam Dalyell at the House of Commons on January 15th, 1985 and the small deputation included the chief constable of West Mercia, Robert Cozens, Detective Chief Superintendent David Cole and another officer. They spent three hours with him. 'They seemed surprised', Dalyell said, afterwards, 'that I had so much information.' He had acquired a large number of files on the subject by that time but, not surprisingly, the one thing that interested them most was the name of Dalyell's source and this, of course, he would not give them.

Afterwards Dalyell published the text of a long letter addressed to Chief Constable Robert Cozens in which he again went through all the points he had made in the House of Commons on December 20th. He emphasised that he had taken the decision to bring the matter before the House during the Consolidated Fund debate after taking advice from senior colleagues and because he had not wanted to see the present home secretary privately. He had not intended any discourtesy to the police whatsoever.

However, he continues:

I really am at a loss to understand how you can really rebuke me for 'hindering' your investigation by making it less likely that witnesses would come forward. After all, your enquiry started on March 24th. I spoke in the Commons on December 19th – *nine* months later. In the meantime your force had some 40,000 records or more and have interviewed a great many people in the Shrewsbury area. Had anyone likely to be deterred by my speech been willing to come forward, surely they would have done so already?

The police, he said, should not be content with bland assurances that intelligence men were not involved, but should cross-question Sir Robert Armstrong (head of the Civil Service and Cabinet Secretary), Mr Peter Mary-church and some of their subordinates – and indeed the head of the security services, the Prime Minister – on how much they have been told and when they were told it. 'Should this not be done, the police will simply have to continue on a time-consuming wild goose chase when they have much else to do.'

Asked if he might have been 'set up', Dalyell replied that he did not think so. 'From one of my sources, seemingly unlikely information on the *Belgrano* turned out to be wholly accurate.' Was the source lying? 'I have no great faith in lie detectors but I'm quite willing to submit to a polygraph test if you think it useful. Perhaps Sir Robert Armstrong, Mr Marychurch and Mrs Margaret Thatcher, who seem to have great faith in polygraphs for other people, would care to submit themselves to the lie detector also if necessary . . .'

He concluded: 'I do not know the identity of Miss Murrell's killer. All I can do is point you in the direction of those who, I believe, can help – and this I have done.'

On Tuesday January 29th, 1985 the police gave their reaction to their meeting with Tam Dalyell and dismissed as speculation the evidence he had put before them. His evidence, said Chief Constable Robert Cozens, amounted to no more than rumour.

In a letter to Mr Dalyell he said: 'A careful assessment of the information, written and oral, that you provided at your interview has now been completed but has produced no evidence to lend substance to your claim that there is a link between the death of Miss Murrell and British Intelligence.' It is clear that Cozens believed that none of the information would lead them to the killer; or be used in a court of law if they found a suspect. 'The written material you gave my officers consists mainly of a collection of speculative articles, letters or remarks from various sources but none of it provides any evidence to support what can best be described as rumours. Regrettably, this also applies to the answers you gave to my officers at your interview.' He pleaded with Dalyell to give him the name of his source. 'I give you my assurance that any evidence that is forthcoming will be thoroughly investigated.'

Tam Dalyell said he had never pretended that the information he would give to the police amounted to evidence. He had told them he did not know the name of the murderer. His source, he said, might be prepared to approach the police after the trial of Clive Ponting.

Whether or not Dalyell had truly hindered the police in their enquiries by intervening some nine months after Hilda Murrell's death, it does appear that during that time there were several important aspects of the case it was left to people other than the police to discover.

When Nick Davies and Martin Bailey broke their story in the *Observer* on January 27th, 1985, that private investigation agencies had been hired to monitor Sizewell objectors – by whoever it was – it seemed the police in West Mercia had not known that this was the case and had certainly made no investigations along those lines.

It also appeared that Rob Green, who was persisting with his own enquiries, had also uncovered a potentially devastating fact. His aunt, he knew, had been working on her paper into the new year of 1984. The draft which was found in her house at the time of her death had been worked on up until some time in February but was not properly completed. As Rob Green had said, he had had to seek assistance from various experts in order to knock it into a shape suitable for reading at the Sizewell enquiry in September. But it does now seem that there had been a properly finished document.

On Sunday March 18th, Hilda Murrell had gone down to her Welsh cottage. While there she had seen a friend, Ms Helen Payling-Wright. Ms Payling-Wright is herself a nuclear physicist but, unlike Hilda Murrell, believed in the need for a nuclear energy programme. However, she had been very helpful to Hilda and had agreed to read over her paper when it was completely finished. Hilda told her on March 18th that her paper was finally 'finished' and that she would be sending her a copy for her comments. The meeting with Ms Payling-Wright was in Hilda Murrell's diary.

On Monday March 19th, Hilda Murrell rang a friend, Mrs Diana Cole. She invited her over the next day for breakfast. This appointment too was in her diary. Over the meal she told Mrs Cole that she had finally finished her paper and how pleased she was about it. After Hilda Murrell's death Mrs Cole was one of those who came forward initially, expressing concern over the possible link between her anti nuclear activities and her death and she was also one of those whose information had been discounted. Unfortunately she became seriously ill and it was not until early in 1985 that she surfaced sufficiently to be able to take an interest again and then she told Rob Green that there had, in fact, been a finished paper, a point later confirmed by Ms Payling-Wright.

So, if there was a finished document in the house, what happened to it?

On January 26th, 1985 there was yet another bizarre twist to the case for during that day Hilda Murrell's Welsh holiday home was burned almost to the ground. It was seen to be on fire at about 8.30 a.m. by a neighbour, who called in the fire brigade. It was afterwards sealed off by police, and forensic scientists were called in from the Home Office laboratories in Chepstow.

Initial reports in the *Shropshire Star* of January 28th, 1985 say most of the damage was to the rear of the timber-framed building but 'it is understood not to be severe'. Rob Green says the bungalow was virtually destroyed.

Evidence was removed for laboratory analysis and a

senior police spokesman told the *Star* the case was being treated as arson. The fire took place just three days after Hilda Murrell's story was featured by Harlech Television in a programme written and researched by John Osmond, who was one of the first journalists to treat the Hilda Murrell story seriously.

Initially, West Mercia police favoured the theory that Welsh arsonists were involved (*Shropshire Star*, January 28th, 1985 and also in conversations with the author) but there are a number of unusual factors about this case not the least of which is that this incident took place during the day.

Both the local police, Dyfed-Powys, and West Mercia are treating it as arson but it appears that Dyfed-Powys police are doubtful about the involvement of Welsh nationalists. Such evidence as they have found does not, apparently, suggest 'holiday home firebombers' and has no hallmark of such a crime (*Wrexham Star*, January 29th, 1985). There seems to be no Welsh political motive behind it nor have any of the Welsh organisations or groups claimed responsibility for it. Both Dyfed-Powys and West Mercia police are asking for possible witnesses.

Tam Dalyell, contacted by the *Wrexham Star* on January 29th, 1985 said he was sure the West Mercia police would do all they could 'and leave no stone unturned to find the cause of the fire . . .' He thought it 'an extraordinary coincidence'.

TEN

A Can of Worms

AT THE time of writing, there has been no arrest in the Hilda Murrell case, now nearly a year old, although developments in this bizarre story seem to continue with every week that passes.

The police case is that they are still committed to finding a burglar, probably a local man, who broke into her house with petty theft in mind and that they hold in their incident room information that makes them sure that cash was the motive for the break-in, information that cannot be revealed. To this end they have made thousands of enquiries and have pulled in at least two petty thieves but neither of them could be charged with the murder of Hilda Murrell.

They have discounted the idea that her death could in any way have been concerned with her anti nuclear activities or with the paper on which she was working for Sizewell.

They have discounted the suggestion that there was anything sinister in the employment of Special Branch on the case. This was routine and the assistance was necessary because of manpower shortages.

They have discounted the *Belgrano* connection or that her death could have come about because somebody thought that her nephew, Rob Green, who had been in naval intelligence during the Falklands conflict, might have passed on to her documents she should not have had.

They have discounted the possibility that British Intelligence officers, from any branch, might have been involved in the break-in. Nothing that Tam Dalyell had to tell them has changed their minds. Yet after a BBC1 *Crimewatch* programme, March 14th, 1985, an anonymous caller claimed that he had worked for MI5 recently. He named someone, who had been hired by MI5, and had committed suicide subsequently, who was responsible for the murder.

They have discounted the suggestion that the burglary at Peter Hurst's flat in St Albans on the night Tam Dalyell was making his speech in the House had anything to do with the Hilda Murrell case although nothing was stolen from the flat and his papers were searched. This is being treated as an ordinary burglary similar to others in the same area but not on the same night.

They say they have no reason to believe there was a finished paper for Sizewell which was no longer in the house after Hilda Murrell's murder.

They have discounted the suggestion that the burning down of her second home in Wales had anything to do with her death and it is being treated as a straight case of arson in an area where there have been other such incidents.

The probing into the mystery surrounding her death by Tam Dalyell and the media has, some eleven months after her death, hindered their enquiries, say the police, and may well have prevented witnesses from coming forward and giving them necessary information. They continue with their search for their burglar.

Those who feel there was more to the break-in, than straight theft are left with many unanswered questions. They include:

1. Why has there been no satisfactory explanation of the discrepancies in the various police accounts of what happened, with what apparently did happen? These include the three versions of when the car number was

fed into the Swansea computer, the 'ransacking' (or not) of the house and the sexual assault (or not) of Hilda Murrell described by Cole on April 19th as 'disgusting'.

2. Why, if the police had eliminated the connection between Hilda Murrell and her anti nuclear activities and her paper for the Sizewell Inquiry, were they still trying to chase up those anti nuclear connections, however ephemeral, as late as October 18th, 1984?

3. If they were still chasing up those anti nuclear connections why did they fail to discover that a private investigation agency was monitoring the Sizewell objectors, when a journalist was able to do so? Not only that, but why was it left to another journalist, Paul Foot, to discover that the man who was eventually contracted to make the enquiries had a long police record for serious offences and had served six years in prison?

4. Were the police aware of the connection between Rob Green and naval intelligence? They must have been. Did they make no enquiries about this or were they too secret to be revealed? Did they check with the intelligence officers we believe were searching for documents connected with the *Belgrano*? Why were they so sure that the burglary of Peter Hurst's flat, so similar to that of Hilda Murrell's house, had no connection with the murder?

5. Why was it left to Rob Green to discover that his aunt appeared to have finished her Sizewell paper but that the finished version was not in her house after her death? The police had already interviewed one of the witnesses.

6. Is the burning down of Hilda's Welsh holiday home a coincidence?

7. Was her body left in a ditch, where, it is suggested, it was seen? If so, then it was afterwards moved to the copse some short time before discovery on March 24th, 1984. If this is so, then Mr Scott would not have seen it on the 22nd, because it would not have been there. Someone came back to 'tidy up' and move it.

There have been too many coincidences in this story.
The first is the fact that a burglar just happened to break
in to Hilda Murrell's house in search of money, was inter-
rupted, attacked her and then dumped her six miles from
home in the copse in the middle of an open field, just at
the time she had finished her paper on Sizewell and should
have been out for the day. The second coincidence is the
link between her and her nephew in naval intelligence and
the sinking of the *Belgrano*. This coincidence includes the
allegations that at the time of her death, frantic efforts
were being made to find missing documents connected
with the *Belgrano*.

The third coincidence is that the Sizewell objectors were
being monitored by at least one detective agency hired by
an unknown employer. By another coincidence, the flat of
a colleague of Robert Green's just happened to be burgled.
And the last coincidence of all is that her holiday home
has now been burned down. There are at least six major
coincidences in this one small story.

But even if the story of Hilda Murrell is no more than
one of police muddle and lots of coincidences and even if
her murderer is, as Dr Peter Acland believes, sitting smugly
in a Shropshire pub laughing and gloating over the media
interest in his repellent murder of a seventy-eight-year-old
rose grower, her death has – if nothing else – opened a
real can of worms.

It is a measure of the climate of opinion in that it is now
believable that the break-in to her home, whoever ordered
it, whoever carried it out and for whatever reasons, could
have had political overtones. For it is a climate where, in
these days of confrontation politics, perfectly respectable
ordinary objectors to a particular policy are seen as subversive, if not 'the enemy within', and therefore have to
be monitored by the secret services.

The investigation into Hilda Murrell's death has been
running parallel to the House of Commons Home Affairs
Select Committee's investigation into the workings of the

Special Branch. Unfortunately as has already been said, this is not going well. Many chief constables are, to put it mildly, reluctant to discuss anything with the Committee. The Home Office is antagonistic. According to one of the Committee members, even the Conservative members of the Committee seem unhappy about pressing anybody for any information at all and they voted out the suggestion that actual serving officers should be called before the Committee and questioned. The terms of reference of the Committee sound fine – 'The Special Branch as part of the police service, its role and accountability' – but no title, however grandiose, is sufficient.

We have already quoted some of the chief constables who have given evidence before the Committee.

The details of those terms of reference sound fine too – that the Special Branch is alleged to be taking an unjustified interest in people carrying out a wide range of lawful activities; that methods of surveillance, including telephone tapping, are carried out either outside agreed law and/or practice without relevant legal safeguards at all; that there is insufficient care or control to establish the relevance, accuracy or currency of information recorded and stored; that those on whom such records are kept have no means of correcting or expunging inaccurate or irrelevant material and so on.

As the National Council for Civil Liberties (NCCL) put to one session of the Select Committee:

Parliament has the most minimal policy or practical scrutiny of Special Branch that could be imaginable. Although the Home Office puts in a budget in relation to Special Branch, this is never questioned and the basis on which the money is spent is never set out in detail. MPs questions in relation to the Special Branch are seldom answered and if they are, there is not sufficient detail given to be able to form any clear analysis. Even the review by this Home Affairs Select Committee, welcome as it is, is likely not to get the kind of information to enable it to come up with coherent proposals in relation to Special Branch.

In short, there is a wholly insufficient amount of public knowledge, control or accountability in relation to Special Branch policy of activities. It is of some importance to observe that seldom has there been any meaningful substantive debate in relation to Special Branch in Parliament. It may be quite rightly argued that there are certain issues and certain information which it would be inappropriate to place before public forums. However, it is difficult to concede that the kind of information kept by Special Branch or even the ground rules within which they operate should not be discussed.

The NCCL goes on to say that it is 'only right and proper' that the Committee should be given information about the kind of individuals and organisations who warrant the attention of the Special Branch

. . . and upon whom files and information are kept. While it is often said that if someone has nothing to hide they have no reason to be concerned about the activity of Special Branch, we think this is not an accurate reflection of the ground rules that Society should hold for Special Branch. Rather, at any time an individual is kept under surveillance and information is kept on file about him or her, it is a violation of personal privacy. Moreover, where information that is kept is inaccurate, irrelevant or out of date, the person can be the subject of police attention or have their immigration status damaged, or have their employment status undermined, sometimes without their knowledge. It cannot be right to assume that Special Branch should be entitled to keep records on any individual it so chooses, irrespective of whether that individual is likely to be engaged in any unlawful activity.

Questions to Council members of local government police authorities from the Select Committee have produced responses such as 'we have no power whatsoever to ask the chief constable to supply records of operational matters at all'; and in answer to the question 'Do you know how many files each Special Branch area actually has?', Councillor R. A. Darrington, chairman of the West Yorkshire police authority answered the Committee on November 28th, 1984 with a simple 'no'.

Councillor E. I. Bentley of the West Midlands, brought up the case of Mrs Madeleine Haigh at that same session, a case very similar to that of Hilda Murrell in that she was a perfectly legitimate anti-nuclear protester. He told the Committee that after Mrs Haigh had written her anti Cruise missile letter to her local paper, it was picked out by a Special Branch officer who gave it as his opinion 'that Mrs Haigh might be the type of person who could be involved in moves which could possibly be termed as "moves against the state". I am concerned,' continued Councillor Bentley, 'that an officer had that criterion and that an officer who could have read a newspaper report can decide to investigate the case.'

Hilda Murrell, too, had written many letters to newspapers in her campaign against the PWR at Sizewell B, including a lengthy correspondence with a member of the UKAEA conducted through the letters column of the *Guardian*.

Concern over the role of the Special Branch, particularly in regard to the 1984/85 miners' strike and fuelled by a number of individual cases, prompted Labour MP John Prescott to write to Home Secretary Leon Brittan asking, among other things, for his detailed view of what constitutes 'subversion'.

On January 28th, 1985 Leon Brittan replied that subversive activities are defined as 'those which threaten the safety or well being of the State, and which are intended to undermine or overthrow Parliamentary democracy by political, industrial or violent means', but that he himself had made it clear in the House of Commons that 'the definition is not limited to possible acts of a criminal nature. In an open society such as ours it is all too easy to use tactics which are not themselves unlawful for subversive ends . . .' He did not accept that this definition allows 'Special Branches to make what you refer to as "political judgements" . . .'

Hilda Murrell's death has also brought out into the light of day the activities of MI5's AIA group with its blanket brief to break the law by entering buildings and searching for whatever it is they might deem of interest to them.

Her death has also shone a spotlight on that really murky world of private surveillance agencies and their tie-ups with Special Branch, security services and, indeed, the Home Office itself.

At the beginning of February 1985 the *Observer*, following its investigations into the agencies which were monitoring Sizewell objectors, handed to the New Scotland Yard anti corruption squad CIB 2, a twenty-eight-page dossier on the workings of some of those groups, claiming that they worked as a 'secret army' for government departments carrying out surveillance, illegal bugging and break-ins, that they bought and sold personal information from official computers – including highly confidential Special Branch files – and that they attended official military intelligence seminars where surveillance techniques were disclosed, even though they had no security clearance. The *Observer*'s Nick Davies writing on February 3rd, 1985 said that the paper had identified a minority of some thirty members of the Institute of Professional Investigators (IPI) currently serving in civilian or military intelligence as well as service police officers and members of the Post Office Investigations Division. The allegations were made to the

Observer by people formerly within the IPI who are certainly in a position to know.

They claim that Special Branch and intelligence officers use these people to do 'dirty work' and provide confidential information in return. Information from Special Branch files, it is claimed, has been on sale among IPI members. If private investigators have the right contacts, the information is there for them to take. Mr Gary Murray, a director of IPI in 1982 told the *Observer*: 'I have sat on a park bench with an operational controller from MI5 and given him the name of a particular individual and said I wanted details on him. He has written it down in his Ministry of Defence notebook and come back to me with what I wanted.'

Mr Murray had attended a surveillance school where 'we were given lessons in interviewing, interrogation and surveillance and told that some of what we would hear was sensitive and shouldn't be repeated. But there were people there with no security clearance at all.' Seminars were held, among other places at the RAF Security School at Newton, Nottingham, and at the Royal Military Police School in Chichester where there were firearms and explosives demonstration. The IPI admit that the seminars were held.

So if, as we said in the chapter on surveillance, Hilda Murrell was being watched then there is a very wide range of choice as to who could have been doing it, at what level it was authorised and who it was who broke into her house.

In his book on the murder of Kenneth Lennon, Geoffrey Robertson says:

The dangers of allowing independent agencies untrammelled power to exploit their custody of national security has recently been illustrated in the United States of America. The CIA, who work closely with the British intelligence services, have been found guilty of numerous breaches of their mandate, including assassination plots . . . and operating a vast network of illegal domestic surveillance. These activities were, for the most part, carried out without executive approval, under the global excuse of national security . . .

'National security' is a magic wand that tends to anaesthetise opposition – and those entrusted with waving it have a power more menacing than can be found in any state. When there is no public accountability, the danger lies in the definition: the Special Branch idea of national security may not coincide with that of Mr Wilson (who was then prime minister) or Mrs Thatcher (who was then leader of the opposition) and even when it does, their operational plans for achieving the desired ends may involve methods that no civilised society could tolerate.

Many of those of us who have been involved in investigating Hilda Murrell's death have received comments and letters pointing to an analogy between it and the murder by the Polish police of Father Popieluszko. While nobody thinks that the men who ended up in court charged with his murder – and who no doubt carried it out – are the only people who were involved and that it was not authorised at a high level, they make the point that at least the men did finally get to court and with the world's media allowed in. This is not Poland, but will it get that far here, they ask?

Robin Gedye writing in the *Daily Telegraph* at the end of the trial in February 1985 said: 'The dark and murky world of Eastern Europe's secret police may never recover from the buffeting it has received in a tiny courtroom in the Polish city of Torun over the past weeks.' Some of the comments he passed on 'the Polish Special Branch' are instructive.

He says that the trial 'has revealed that the Special Branch blatantly flaunts the law if it believes a "higher moral order" will thereby be served.' He also writes that: 'The trial has shown up a bumbling, inefficient, occasionally amateurish secret police world . . .' He concludes his summary of the Popieluszko trial by saying that 'whatever the outcome, and few people believe any of the accused will be let off lightly, the Polish security services will never be the same again.'

But probably a stronger parallel with the murder of Hilda Murrell is that of the death of Karen Silkwood. Silkwood was the employee of the Kerr-McGee plutonium plant in the United States who met her death in mysterious circumstances. She had campaigned for a long time about what she considered was the wholesale neglect of safety standards at the plant which exposed employees to high levels of radiation. She was working on a dossier to prove her point. Several days before she died, she was mysteriously irradiated with plutonium to the point that her family had to bury her in a new dress because all the clothes she possessed were so contaminated that they had to be buried, with the rest of her effects, in a sealed container.

Aware of what had happened, she set out with her dossier to meet a journalist from the *New York Times* and a representative of her union from its Washington head office. She never completed the journey. On November 13th, 1974, Karen Silkwood's car was forced off the road on a motorway and she died in the crash. Her papers were never found and the dossier has not turned up to this day.

The full force of the United States establishment then turned on Karen Silkwood accusing her of being emotionally disturbed, sexually promiscuous and hooked on drugs. But as Richard Rashke says of her in his book *The Killing of Karen Silkwood* (Sphere Books 1984). 'She was no mystery. In life she was an ordinary woman who stuck her neck out. In death she became a nuclear martyr.'

Among the questions he says may never be answered about her death are: what was in the documents, what happened to them and was she murdered?

Nobody can blacken Hilda Murrell's character as they attempted to do to Karen Silkwood. She was elderly, respectable and respected. She opposed one aspect of government policy but she did so most openly and in the approved democratic way. She did not participate in demonstrations, illegal or legal, nor did she believe in breaking the law. Fortuitously, she had a close relative who had been in naval intelligence and who had connections with another sensitive issue, that of the Falklands War. She was working on a paper which she was about to read at the Sizewell public enquiry, for all to hear.

Dr Peter Acland might like to imagine his scenario of Hilda's murderer gloating in a pub, but there could be another – that of a couple of secret service men, or a couple of private investigators doing exactly the same thing while their superiors were left to cover up the mess. From the end of March until the beginning of November they looked, if this notion is a possibility, as if they were going to get away with it. Nothing more would be heard about the death of Hilda Murrell and, eventually, her file would sink quietly into the category of unsolved murders. The local press accepted the police explanation without question and nobody else was interested. That would have been that.

A year later Hilda Murrell's story has been told not only by nearly every section of the British media but has featured in publications all over the world. She is rapidly passing into mythology as another possible nuclear martyr.

As in the case of Karen Silkwood it is optimistic to think we will ever know the answers to some of the most vital questions. Who murdered her? What were they looking for? Did they find it? Who authorised the break-in? But that is no reason for not trying to discover the truth.

At a period when informed democratic dissent no longer has any legitimacy and a respectable protester against a power programme which many consider to be unwise can be considered as a subversive, then it has become believable that, during a break-in, a 'tragic accident' could occur and such a protester could, in fact, become expendable.

Timetable

25. 2.1984	Hilda Murrell tells Morgan-Grenville of fears for safety.
12. 3.1984	Campbells are told Hilda fears for her personal safety.
18. 3.1984	Hilda tells Helen Payling-Wright she has finished her Sizewell paper.
20. 3.1984	Hilda has Diana Cole to her home and tells her her paper is finished.
21. 3.1984	10.30 a.m. approximately: Hilda leaves home for shops. 12.00 p.m.: Speaks to neighbour and goes back into house. 12.30 p.m. approximately: Her white Renault 5 seen being driven erratically out of Shrewsbury. 1.20 p.m. Car seen in ditch at Hunkington. 2.00–2.20 approximately: Running man seen between lane leading to Hunkington, and Shrewsbury. Mid afternoon: abandoned car reported to police. Afternoon (time not known): two thieves take tax disc off car.

22. 3.1984   3.00 p.m.: Scott walks through copse, sees no body.
4.00 p.m.: dark car seen near copse. Man gets out walks over to copse and returns to car.
Evening: Lights seen in copse.

23. 3.1984   9.00 a.m.: gardener finds kitchen door open to Hilda's house. Light on in kitchen, curtains drawn.
10.30 a.m.: car again reported to police.
During morning: Red Escort seen driving backwards and forwards along lane near copse.
6.30 p.m.: policeman calls at Hilda's, knocks and goes away.
6.30–7.00 p.m.: police call on sexual counsellor.
Neighbours say police in house during evening. Police deny this.

24. 3.1984   6.30 a.m.: policeman calls at house again.
9.00 a.m.: gardeners arrive.
10.30 a.m.: Rob Green rings his aunt, receives no reply.
10.30 a.m: Hilda Murrell's body found in copse.

26. 3.1984   First police major press statement. House 'ransacked', etc.

3. 4.1984   Police begin contacting Hilda's anti nuclear contacts.

18. 4.1984   Thieves who stole tax disc appear in court.

19. 4.1984	Police release statement on 'sexual attack' on Hilda Murrell.
28. 6.1984	One West Mercia officer suspended. Newspaper report says he played golf while on duty investigating case. One officer from West Midlands suspended likewise.
2. 8.1984	Third police officer suspended.

Sometime around end July/beginning August: Peter X arrested, not charged and then released.

3. 8.1984	Rob Green told suddenly to collect Hilda's body for burial. Told there was second autopsy on 25.7.1984
18. 8.1984	*Guardian* report on Hilda's death and her Sizewell paper.
25. 8.1984	Hilda's body is finally cremated.
13. 9.1984	Hilda's paper read at the Sizewell enquiry.
18.10.1984	Police still contacting nuclear connections in spite of denials.
9.11.1984	*New Statesman* breaks story on Hilda Murrell.
20.12.1984	Tam Dalyell makes statement in the House of Commons.
20.12.1984	Flat of Peter Hurst, only other naval intelligence officer to resign from Northwood since Falklands War, colleague of Rob Green, has his flat broken into. Nothing stolen but papers searched.

8. 1.1985   *Standard* story reveals professional burglar questioned on Murrell case is frightened of being framed. It later transpires a second man was similarly questioned.

15. 1.1985   Police visit Tam Dalyell at House of Commons.

17. 1.1985   Giles Shaw's statement on Dalyell's questions. Also says security services not involved.

26. 1.1985   Hilda Murrell's Welsh holiday home is burned to the ground. Police say it is arson but Welsh Nationalists are not necessarily suspected.

27. 1.1985   *Observer* breaks story on Sizewell objectors being kept under surveillance by detective agency for private client.

31. 1.1985   Paul Foot breaks story that private detective was man with criminal record. Police say they know nothing of this.

Official position	*Discrepancies*
21.3.1984 Hilda Murrell's car first reported, again 23.3.1984. Police state to author (and others) car was examined, nothing wrong, treated as abandoned vehicle until 23.3.1984.	In fact there are 3 police versions: 1. Rob Green told April 1984 wrong number put in Swansea computer. 2. Author and press told version as opposite. Quoted in NS 9.11.1984, also inquest 5.12.1984. 3. On 17.1.1985 Giles Shaw tells House of Commons police put correct number in Swansea computer immediately on 21.3.1984.
26.3.1984 Police release press statement on murder saying house 'ransacked'.	House was not ransacked, but systematically searched, papers gone through. 17.1.1985 Police deny having said it was ransacked.

Police deny entry into Hilda Murrell's home during evening of 23.3.1984 on many occasions.

Witnesses saw police in house on that evening. Numerous reports including 9.11.1984.

Police say they forced entry into her house on morning of 24.3.1984, 26.3.1984 et al.

Gardener found back door unlocked on 23.3.1984. Policeman found door unlocked on evening of 23.3.1984 and also at 6.30 a.m. on 24.3.1984.

Police say phone cut off in a professional manner. 18.8.1984 et al.

Police do not deny this until Giles Shaw's statement to House 17.1.1985. Now say wires just wrenched out.

Police say Hilda Murrell sexually assaulted. 19.4.1984. Statement from Cole to that effect and that forensic evidence proved it.

Shaw's statement 17.1.1985. Police now deny she was sexually assaulted.

Police say body was in copse since death. Repeated at inquest 5.12.1984.

Scott visits copse 22.3.1984. Sees no body there. Also possible other witness to body not being there.

Police say nuclear connection discounted. Told author so mid-October and frequently since.

Enquiries into nuclear connection commenced 3.4.1984 still going on 18.10.1984 (letters as proof).

Flat of only other naval officer to resign from Northwood since Falklands War broken into 20.12.1984. Nothing stolen but papers searched.

Police say ordinary burglary, could not be connected with *Belgrano* or Murrell case.

Police say all Hilda's papers are still in house after death. Have said so all along.

Rob Green discovers in March 1984 that she had finished her paper on Sizewell and that it is missing.

General Inconsistencies

Police denied throughout that Special Branch was involved.

December 1984 chief constable of West Mercia states they were called in on 'routine basis' as police force short of manpower.

Police and then coroner refused to release post mortem reports on two autopsies saying it is up to coroner's discretion. This repeated by Shaw.

This, according to 'inquest' reading of *Halsbury's Rules for Coroners* appears to be quite incorrect.

Police say all possible leads on murder were followed up.

They were not aware of private agencies being involved in surveillance of Sizewell objectors. 19.1.1985.

The person who broke into the house, attacked Hilda Murrell, searched carefully through her papers and then drove her six miles away from her home, leaving her to die in a field and stole only fifty pounds cash is an ordinary burglar.

Chief Supt. Cole at inquest 5.12.1984 says he has evidence to prove this in his incident room but cannot reveal what it is.

Appendix

I

Sizewell B Power Station Public Enquiry
An Ordinary Citizen's View of
Radioactive Waste Management
by
Hilda Murrell MA
(To be read at the enquiry by Mr R. Green)

Introductory Statement at Presentation of Proof

My name is Robert Green. During the 1970s my late aunt
Miss Hilda Murrell became interested in what she saw as
the unacceptable hazards of nuclear power generation.
She read the Department of the Environment's White
Paper Cmnd 8607 soon after it was published in 1982, and
wrote a critique of it which was then found to be relevant
to this Enquiry. Having incorporated some points arising
at the Enquiry on March 7th, 1984 she applied to read her
Proof of Evidence personally as the first individual and
completely independent objector on this aspect.

However, on March 21st she was murdered by an as yet
unknown intruder into her home in an act of seemingly
mindless violence.

Besides being her nephew, I knew her well and agreed

with her views on the civil nuclear industry. She therefore kept me informed on the progress of her paper. I retired from the Royal Navy as a commander in 1982 under voluntary redundancy and am now training in Dorset to be a thatcher. I am self-employed with a small service pension, and am thus able to present her proof, which expresses the major concern of her final years. In such tragic and probably unprecedented circumstances, it is now my overriding concern that her untimely death should not be allowed to prevent her views from being heard in the way that she had wished.

Hilda Murrell was born in 1906 in Shrewsbury, where she lived all her life; and she was educated at Shrewsbury high school and Newnham College, Cambridge, where she read English, Modern and Mediaeval Languages, and French.

Her grandfather Edwin founded a rose nursery, and she joined the family firm in 1928 after graduating from Cambridge. In its final years the company was under her sole management until she sold it in 1970 and retired. By then she had become an international authority on rose species, old varieties and miniature roses.

Her deep love and concern for the countryside and wildlife, as well as her botanical expertise, made her an active founder-member of the Shropshire Conservation Trust in 1962, and she also worked for the Shropshire branch of CPRE. She was a founder-member of the Soil Association. Her experience and knowledge of conservation of the environment thus drew her to investigate the impact upon it posed by the nuclear industry.

An Ordinary Citizen's View of
Radioactive Waste Management
by
Hilda Murrell, MA

Introduction

1. An Ordinary Citizen with a typical middle-class, sub-urban and small business-management background, read the Department of the Environment's White Paper Cmnd 8607, decided it was very unsatisfactory, and wrote a critique of it. Later a friend pointed out that it was relevant to the Sizewell B Inquiry. Transcripts were sent for, and this was found to be so; they also raised points which called for further comments, and these have now been incorporated in the original paper.

Some Comments on the White Paper Cmnd 8607, Radio-active Waste Management

2. This paper was issued by the Secretary of State for the Environment and the Secretaries of State for Scotland and Wales in July 1982.

3. *White Paper (WP) Subparagraph 3(iv)*. This last sentence reads: 'Throughout, the public must be kept fully informed about what is being done, and there must be proper scope for public discussion.'

4. Hear, hear. The whole nuclear enterprise was started, and has continued, in closely guarded secrecy, and hundreds of millions of pounds of Ordinary Citizens' money have been spent on it without their knowledge let alone consent, or Parliament being involved at all. Only little by little has it been possible for them to realise the extent of this commitment and the seriousness of the issues raised by it. That such a thing could be done in a democratic country on a matter of such importance is highly disturbing. The Ordinary Citizen is entitled to complete frankness from now on.

5. If the government really means this statement that 'the public must be kept fully informed', its reports should be free. The nuclear question is unique in its importance to the Ordinary Citizen and the future of this country. £2.85 for this pamphlet of 18 pages is out of proportion to the average income. To get all the others quoted in Cmnd 8607 as well is financially impossible. The Central Electricity Generating Board (CEGB)'s Annual Report should be free – last year they started asking for payment. To people who are enforced shareholders and consumers of this monopolistic corporation, that is intolerable. All this information should be accessible even to the poorest.

6. *WP Paragraph 7 and Fig 1*. The first sentence reads: 'One basic characteristic of radioactivity, which *actually assists in waste management*, is that it decays over time.'

7. But it is precisely the 'decay' of unstable elements which *is* the radioactive event, and which therefore poses all the ensuing problems. To say that decay 'actually assists in waste management' is to stand the whole situation on its head, and is unbelievably fatuous.

8. Many of these very dangerous elements would never have existed at all but for man's meddling with the very building-blocks of the universe. Nor do they disappear to nothingness, as the word 'decay' might imply. They form decay-products (not even mentioned here) which are also sometimes radioactive, and may even work through a

important paragraph.

whole series of them before reaching a state of stability. Some of these are more dangerous than the elements from which they started. For the same reason, the graph is meaningless: no elements are named on it.

9. The bright and cheery thought conveyed by the quotation is as pure an example of 'newspeak' as could be found. Windscale into Sellafield is another. The deep mental dishonesty they betray is terrifying.

10. On Day 100, para 10B, Mr Wedd of the Department of the Environment (DoE), while admitting that the fact of their radioactivity sets such wastes apart from all others, tried to make out that their decay is a point in their favour, a 'plus' in comparison with arsenic, mercury, cyanide, etc, a 'time dimension' he called it. Plutonium-239 with a half-life of 24,413 years hardly peters out in a 'time dimension' that can readily even be imagined. Far less can such slow decay provide any practical advantage in its management compared with the above 'conventional' elements. Just one quarter of its first half-life alone puts it beyond any possibility of our being able to guarantee its isolation from all living things, which is essential. This watering down and minimising of extremely serious problems is precisely what promotes instead of allays the uneasiness of the public, whose reaction is therefore rational, not emotional, as is so often made out.

11. Arsenic, mercury, etc, existed before man and will exist after him. He is not responsible for their being here. This is not to say that he should use them in such a way as to make them too easily accessible, which does happen. Man, on the other hand, creates the radioactive pollutants which emerge from nuclear power-stations in unprecedented number, concentration and violence. *He need not do it.*

12. *WP Paragraph 8.* Sentence 2 reads: 'An estimated 78 per cent of the radiation received by the population of the United Kingdom is from natural sources, and a further 21 per cent from medical uses. The amount received from all

other uses is very small, about 1 per cent, and the amount caused by the discharge of radioactive wastes to the environment is only 0.1 per cent of the total.'

13. The sources of background radiation usually mentioned are cosmic rays, and the granite rock of which the earth's crust is formed. Cosmic rays tend to concentrate at the magnetic poles. The inhabitants of Aberdeen and Cornwall, where the granite comes to the surface, are not commonly seen chewing pieces of their native rock: for it is the *ingestion* of radioactive elements that constitutes the main danger. As man is not infallible, some of the very large and concentrated quantities of radioactive material accumulated in thirty-odd years by the industry do escape, both in constant small seepages and occasionally, in spite of all care, in accidents, and it is difficult, if not impossible, to prevent their entering the food-chain. A steady build-up continues. Once it gets into the sea, for instance, strontium 89 or 90, with its affinity to calcium, lodges in the lime structure of minute foraminifera, which are consumed by larger creatures and so on upwards to the fish which are eaten by man. The strontium is concentrated in the food chain at every step.

14. To express the nuclear industry's contribution to these ratios in terms only of what it is considered safe to discharge is a gross distortion of the situation. If one year's total production of radioactivity from the industry were put in instead, the proportions would be startlingly different: but this is the quota which is the real contribution to the existing sources of radiation. All this on top of thirty years' accumulation of the more long-lasting and dangerous high-level wastes (HLW). The fact that it has to be completely contained with scrupulous care and at increasing cost does not alter this. It is possibly the worst form of industrial pollution ever created by man, unique in its combination of intense and continuing heat with toxicity and radioactive penetration. It contains a whole range of transuranic actinides which do not occur in nature. The

world's burden of radioactivity from this source is being increased at a disturbing rate every year. Once created it cannot be destroyed, and there is as yet no acceptable form of final disposal, as opposed to management, in sight anywhere (a matter to which I will return). This country has the greatest concentration of nuclear installations for its size and crowded population of any in the world. A table showing last year's total arisings, including of course Windscale, in terms of radioactivity from the industry, would have been a more seemly contribution than this, from a body having responsibility for these wastes. The Ordinary Citizen would also be glad to know exactly what emissions are included in this 0.1 per cent.

15. *WP Paragraph 10*. The International Commission on Radiological Protection (ICRP) has twice already in its history lowered the prescribed limits for radiation dose, so one is bound to keep a very open mind about the present ones. They are now under challenge once again.

16. In his Proof of Evidence to the Enquiry on behalf of DoE (DoE/P/2 Para 3.1) Mr Hookway says: 'The ICRP set upper limits of radiation exposure for workers and the public. Limits for workers are set by comparison with the risks of other occupations having high standards of safety'. In DoE/P/2(Add2) page 3, he tells us that this means occupations where the death-rate per annum does not exceed 100 per million in that occupation, and he follows this with a table setting out examples of one year in America, date not given.

17. A useful addition to the table would be the death-rate from lung cancer among uranium miners, resulting from radiation-carrying dust. They were very light-hearted about these hazards in the early days of uranium mining in America, and the US Public Health Service has estimated that between 600 and 1,100 out of 6,000 men who worked at it in those days would die of lung cancer. Taking an even-bottom figure of 750 from this estimate gives a death-rate of 125,000 per million. Decreasing this by a

factor of 10 to allow for improvements in conditions (ventilation of mines, etc) gives 12,500 per million, which is practically four times the total figure given by Mr Hookway (3148 × 4 = 12,592), and is over twelve times the death-rate he gives for mining. Presumably he means coal mining.

18. The whole nuclear industry rests on this ghastly base. On top of this hazard are the thousands of tons of tailings resulting from the milling of the rock to extract the uranium, which is done near the mine. These tailings are in the form of fine dry sand containing radium and its deadly decay-products, which will be blown about the whole area for thousands of years. It would be refreshing never to be told again (as we so often have been) that nuclear power is so clean and safe compared with coal-mining.

19. With regard to Mr Hookway's second table on the same page (accident liability), it should be emphasised heavily that an accident involving radioactivity is entirely different in kind from the ones listed, which are limited to the time, the place and the people concerned. A radio-active accident reaches, sometimes vastly, beyond all these. To compare it with an 'ordinary' accident, however disastrous, is to compare things that are non-comparable.

20. Mr Hookway says on page 2 of DoE/P/2 that the ICRP sets upper limits for the public 'in the light of public acceptance of other risks in everyday life'. What sort of standard is this? Not what is right, but what they will stand!

21. Here we have embodied, almost as a principle, the shocking but frequently used non-argument (another which it would be a mercy to be spared henceforth) that because people put up with 6,000 road deaths a year, or other existing horror, why worry about a little more danger from nuclear power (especially as the deaths from this don't occur until ten, fifteen or twenty years later, so responsibility can be evaded)? One evil does not justify another, and the opposite conclusion should be drawn, that both evils should be abolished, or at the very least that another should not be added.

22. When the case for nuclear power has to be propped up by such shoddy arguments as these, the Ordinary Citizen concludes that it can't be very good: hence his mistrust of the people using them increases accordingly.

23. *WP Paragraph 12.* To illustrate my point further, para 12 is worth quoting in full:

> The government attaches great importance to the safe and effective management of radioactive wastes. As a result of research undertaken in this and other countries over the last five years, there is no evidence of any major scientific problems and the government has concluded that it is feasible to manage and dispose of all the wastes currently envisaged in the UK, in acceptable ways. There is an extensive body of existing knowledge about the technology involved. In some respects this will have to be further refined and developed, and the necessary work is in hand. The main task, however, is to identify the most appropriate of the methods available to us for each category of waste, and then ensure that this method is implemented according to an agreed programme and in a way that meets the objectives for radiological protection.

24. Now contrast what the Royal Commission on Environmental Pollution said in para 338 of its 1976 Report on Nuclear Power:

> . . . there should be no commitment to a large programme of nuclear fission power until it has been demonstrated beyond reasonable doubt that a method exists to ensure the safe containment of long-lived, highly radioactive waste for the indefinite future. These wastes already exist in considerable quantity . . . and a safe method for their long-term disposal is in any case required whatever is decided about nuclear development

in the future. We are clear that such a demonstration
will require a substantial programme of research.

It effectively repeats this in paras 181 and 533, emphasising
that any other course would be 'irresponsible and morally
wrong'. This thrice-repeated statement of principle is one
of its most important conclusions. It is a minimum requirement, and makes the government's statement that 'there
is no evidence of any scientific problems' and its confident
conclusion (reiterated even more stridently in the last
sentence of para 24) ring hollow in the ordinary citizen's
ears.

25. *WP Paragraph 13*. In 1977 DoE, having taken over
responsibility for waste management, set out its aims in a
White Paper, and I would like to draw attention to two of
them from the list quoted here:

    a. Subparagraph 13(ii): 'ensure that waste manage-
    ment problems are dealt with before any large nuclear
    programme is undertaken'; and

    b. Subparagraph 13(vi): 'secure the disposal of wastes
    in appropriate ways at appropriate times and in appro-
    priate places.'

26. At least we have here a grudging acknowledgment that
the Royal Commission was right to emphasise that there is
a problem after all. But note how the Royal Commission's
statement of aims has been emasculated in DoE's version.
In subpara 13(ii), '. . . ensure that waste management
problems are dealt with . . .' is substituted for '. . . there
should be no commitment . . . until it has been demonstrated beyond reasonable doubt that a method exists to
ensure the safe containment of long-lived highly radioactive waste for the indefinite future . . .', which is not
mentioned at all in the White Paper. In subpara 13(vi),
the disposal of wastes (without specification) is left to
whoever likes to think what is 'appropriate', apparently.
There is total laxity just at the point where the principle
needs to be stressed most strongly.

27. *WP Paragraph 26.* Sentence 2 includes the statement: '. . . those disposal routes which already exist for radioactive wastes are acceptable and should continue to be used, if necessary on an increasing scale.'

28. This is a statement of intention that the government really does mean to put into action. Its prompt rejection of a European vote for a two-year moratorium on ocean dumping of low and not-so-low-activity wastes shows where its priorities lie: nuclear industry a very good first, environment nowhere. I refer back to WP para 12: '. . . the government has concluded that it is feasible to manage and dispose of all the wastes currently envisaged in the UK, in appropriate ways.' The international community does not appear to agree on the acceptableness of this one. The 'conclusion' seems clear, that the government is determined that waste management shall not be a barrier to the further development of nuclear power (see again WP para 24).

29. Britain has done more than 95 per cent of the dumping in the deep Atlantic. A special ship is being built to carry the waste (cost?). So the flouting of the moratorium raises the question of how serious the government is about any good intentions expressed in this White Paper. In this connection, the transport unions who have now put a stop to the practice stand for civilisation, and the government for barbarism.

30. *WP Paragraph 27 and 34.* The Thermal Oxide Reprocessing Plant (THORP) was given planning permission early in 1978. In its report for 1981–82 British Nuclear Fuels Limited said: 'Preparation of the site at Sellafield is at an advanced stage.' Does it really take over three years to do only this? In the meantime we are having to provide storage for the spent oxide fuel, not only from this country, but also from several others, which arrives constantly (see below). Para 27 does not even suggest that there is anything to be dealt with other than our own oxide fuel from the few AGR stations yet working. Imports are just barely

mentioned in para 34, where it says that 'as reprocessing is currently undertaken on a commercial scale only by the UK and Fance, BNFL have been able to acquire valuable additional business by reprocessing spent fuel from other countries.'

31. The only reprocessing which the UK is currently able to do is Magnox. However, it was stated in the *Guardian* on March 6th, 1984, that the Sellafield nuclear reprocessing plant dealt with 321 tonnes of imported spent uranium fuel, from seven different countries last year, according to the junior Energy Minister, Mr Giles Shaw. Uranium came from Japan, Italy, Sweden, Switzerland, Spain, West Germany and the Netherlands. But only two Magnox stations have been sold abroad, one to Japan and one to Italy. The conclusion seems inescapable, that we are also importing spent oxide fuel and simply storing it until THORP becomes operational.

32. The last sentence of para 34 reads: 'All overseas contracts made since 1976 have included an option for BNFL to return the wastes from these operations to the country of origin.' This is unlikely to happen, so we will probably be landed with more vicious HLW than we have already from Magnox.

33. One wonders how valuable any of this business will be by the end of the saga. The outlook is not encouraging. The Americans tried oxide fuel reprocessing and failed miserably, with an escape of radioactive contamination and a considerable cost overrun. The French oxide fuel reprocessing plant at Cap de la Hague has only achieved a fraction of planned capacity. The chances of THORP being able to do any better are a mere gamble. The capital cost of THORP was quoted as £600 million at the Windscale Inquiry in 1976. This did not include interest. BNFL has recently received detailed planning permission from Copeland District Council: in the course of the proceedings the present capital cost was quoted at £2 billion and construction time at 10 years. The cost will surely

have doubled by the end of that time. This plant will be roughly the size of Wembley Stadium. Meanwhile the Japanese contribution of £140 million to the capital cost (which was part of the contract) is shrinking steadily in proportion to this total. If THORP should fail, it is forfeit anyway.

34. It was said at the Sizewell Enquiry in BNFL's Statement of Case that THORP is only counted on to last ten years. It would then itself have to be decommissioned, presumably adding to the so far unsolved problem (a massive one) of solid intermediate level wastes. If it should work, and at a capacity sufficient to justify the enormous capital outlay, it would have to have successors: three in the lifetime of the power stations it was designed to serve, and each costing several times the quoted price of such a station. Has this cost been taken into account by CEGB, which is absolutely certain that the PWR is going to produce electricity more cheaply than coal, and than any other nuclear reactor it has had yet? No businessman in his senses would take on such a proposition as this, so why is it inflicted on the British taxpayer and electricity consumer?

35. At the enquiry (Day 95, para 52D) the DoE witness, Mr Wedd, said under cross-examination: 'There are, of course, a whole string of decisions still required to bring the THORP reprocessing plant into operation, and to decide on its successor when that plant has run its useful course.' If everybody is getting cold feet, it would not be surprising, and would account for the delay; also for the planned provision of storage capacity for eighteen years' spent fuel-rods at Sizewell B, which would seem to indicate an expectation of two THORPs'-worth of teething troubles. So that is where we are, seven years on from the Windscale enquiry.

36. How many successors to THORP Mark I, the size of Wembley Stadium, could Windscale accommodate? With ten years' construction time and a ten-year life, construction on this part of the nuclear cycle would be perpetual

(at billions a time). Are there any possibilities of decontamination and re-use of the sites? Windscale is not limitless, but one cannot imagine a Windscale II being accepted voluntarily anywhere in these islands. At the Windscale enquiry BNFL said it already 'earmarked several sites.' Such a plan could only be imposed by outright dictatorship. Do we really need to come to this for the sake of a fraction of our electricity supply, which could easily and completely wholesomely be provided in other ways (see Day 101, evidence by Mr D Ross)?

37. *WP Paragraphs 28, 32 and 57.* Storage of 'heat-generating' HLW is the worst and possibly most dangerous of all the processes of nuclear waste management. The stainless steel tanks in which they are kept at Windscale cost £4 million each in 1976. The extremely hot and violently radioactive wastes are dissolved in nitric acid. This is the most reactive of the common mineral acids, and also an oxidising agent; so that, if there were ever a leak from these tanks, there would be a danger of fire. If a fire took hold here, the ensuing catastrophe would be worse than a melt-down at a power-station. The twelve tanks are provided with seven separate cooling systems, but there is no alternative general water supply – no fail-safe for this, the most dangerous complex in these islands. Yet para 57 says that this question of HLW '. . . is not an immediate issue'! It is not one perforce, because the next stages of treatment are not ready, and nothing can be done about HLW until they are. To have a system of power-production needing such a devil's brew as this, is just plain silly.

38. Sentence 4 of WP para 28 begins: 'Work is going ahead on the design of a vitrification plant . . .' The possibility of the vitrification of HLW was first mooted in the mid-fifties, and the United Kingdom Atomic Energy Authority (UKAEA) started on it but did hardly anything all through the sixties although the work was known to be urgent. In the seventies the HARVEST vitrification project got going but, before it could be fully tested, the Secretary for

the Environment told Parliament in 1981 that BNFL's 'preference' was to build the first Windscale vitrification plant based on the French AVM process, which had already operated successfully for two years. Preference implies choice; but the French process was (and is) the only one working in the world: so BNFL had *no* choice. The French are hard-headed, and will no doubt make a heavy charge for their expertise; so the Ordinary Citizen will pay twice over for this facility. It is relevant to note here that the money for research and development for UKAEA comes from the Department of Energy's fund for general scientific and industrial R&D [Research and Development], of which it has the lion's share.

39. On para 32, seeing that the main ingredients of HLW (strontium 90 and caesium 137) remain very active for 500 to 600 years, can the assurance expressed in the last sentence about the durability of any materials over several centuries really be justified? The French plant has now been running for only five years. Extreme heat and radiation combined are already seen to be causing embrittlement in materials, and we simply do not know (see also para 43 below).

40. If vitrification should not work we are faced with a dreadful prospect. Mr Wedd of DoE said at the enquiry (DoE/P/1 Add2): 'These wastes remain potentially harmful in proportion to their radiotoxicity and, unless disposed of, would require to be safeguarded indefinitely if they were to remain in liquid form . . . the wastes, however, are only actually harmful if the radioactivity is allowed to affect living things.' That, of course, is actually the whole point of what we are all discussing.

41. The steel tanks in which the HLW are contained are only reckoned to have a life of around thirty years. There are now twelve of them containing about 1,000 m^3 of liquid. So thirty-six per century would be required to deal with present liabilities, or say forty with spares (which are necessary). This would suppose posterity to have 'indefi-

nitely' the technical, financial and social capabilities to produce them.

42. What is intended to be done with the FBR wastes at Dounreay which cannot be concentrated, and for which no vitrification process exists, *even in theory*? (1979 Review of Cmnd 884: 'The Control of Radioactive Wastes', page 55, para 4.16).

43. *WP Paragraph 31*. On geological disposal, evidence given by Dr D. G. Arnott at the Cheviot Borehole Enquiry emphasised that twenty to thirty years' experience of the effects of intense heat and radioactivity combined on any containment material was insufficient for irretrievable disposal to be justified, and that an engineered store would be safer for posterity although requiring supervision for 500 to 600 years. The cogency of this argument, and the reception accorded to the proponents of boreholes by the doughty Northumbrians, resulted in the borehole programme being called off. DoE retreated to their desks and to a review of progress of work abroad on this subject instead. Such work is not always relevant to UK conditions, but in spite of this they have concluded in the light of it that '. . . the emplacement of HLW deep underground . . . is now established in principle . . . and nothing has emerged to indicate that it would be unacceptable' (Third Annual Report of the Radioactive Waste Management Advisory Committee (RWMAC), page 49).

44. The flaw in this 'principle' (held with the greatest tenacity at the Enquiry) does not emerge: it's down there – namely, water. Continental evidence is not suitable as an example for the British Isles, which are constantly saturated with moisture driven in from the Atlantic. It is most unlikely that even the hardest rocks would be free of it. Groundwater contains mineral salts in solution. The corrosive effect of these would combine with and intensify the factors mentioned in the Cheviot evidence. Leakage of radioactivity into the groundwater would be an unmitigated and irreversible disaster.

45. The Institute of Geological Sciences has pronounced on the present state of knowledge and is quoted in Day 95, para 59F–G by Mr Blake of the Town and Country Planning Association (TCPA) in cross-examination of Mr Wedd of DoE:

> The type of information required to assess the geological barrier provided by various formations is largely unavailable. For example, with respect to crystalline rocks, geologists have tended to be concerned more with their petrology and mode of formation than with their hydrogeological properties or the geochemistry of groundwater systems within them. The hydrogeology of poorly permeable rocks in general is a subject which has been neglected by scientists because previously there was little application for such information.

And in para 60D: 'Site-specific feasibility at a level leading to an acceptable safety analysis has not been demonstrated anywhere in the world.'

46. They are quoted again in para 61D: 'The basis of reliability for any assessment is the degree of confidence placed in predictions extended to very long periods in the future. Realistic groundwater flow and transport models have yet to be validated in the field in any country.'

47. And RWMAC's Fourth Report, para 6.26 (quoted in para 64D) says: 'So far as geological disposal is concerned the main function of backfilling and sealing will be to prevent or retard vertical upward movement of groundwater, which would be the shortest pathway back to man. This presents a technically very difficult task.'

48. Can a project where the main problems have barely been researched at all, anywhere, really be said to be 'established in principle'?

49. At the mention of final disposal of HLW under the ocean bed, the horse-sense of the ordinary citizen rebels completely. Our contribution to research into this method

of disposal was £3 million in 1982–83 (DoE/P/1, para 6.12). What sort of system of energy-production is this, which on top of all the extraordinary, dangerous, exceedingly expensive and barely half-tried stratagems already mentioned, has to resort to such a desperate measure as this – and all just to try to get rid of the rubbish? And all after the main job of electricity generation itself? The difficulties and dangers met with in oil drilling on the continental shelf would be compounded in the ocean deeps, as would the cost. How can nuclear power possibly be anything but many times dearer than any other system of energy-production ever devised?

50. Mr Wedd says (Day 95, para 64H) that the main effort is now directed to 'bringing the state of knowledge of the sea and under-sea options to the same level as the land options'; but he admits that the feasibility of these has not been established even in principle.

51. On Day 100, para 10G–H, in answer to objectors who say that we should not create substances which we do not know how to get rid of, he says: 'There are no such substances to our knowledge in the radioactive waste field. They can all be managed, held in storage and disposed of safely within the limits of present knowledge and present technology.'

52. One can only suppose that Mr Wedd has means of reconciling such statements with those of the geologists and his own RWMAC which are denied to the ordinary citizen. He has said himself that the sea options have not even been researched or 'established in principle' at all.

53. When asked whether this state of the art satisfies the principle of ensuring that 'waste management problems are dealt with before any large nuclear programme is undertaken', he is completely convinced that it does. He says (Day 95, para 66D):

the phrase 'dealt with' does not mean that one should have shown that one can now do something that will not be possible to be done for the period of 50 years. It should show either (*sic*) that the problems that arise now, and can be dealt with now, are within the compass of normal technology and administration, and that there is good reason to suppose that the problems that will arise in fifty years' time will be within the compass of present technology.

Perhaps the missing alternative should be 'or not'.

54. The Royal Commission asks for demonstration 'beyond reasonable doubt that a method exists to ensure the safe containment of long-lived, highly radioactive waste for the indefinite future'. Neither THORP nor the vitrification plant yet exists, nor do the following stages, and neither is what one would put under the heading of either 'normal technology' or 'normal administration'.

55. *WP Paragraph 35.* With regard to the quantity of intermediate level wastes, the DoE witness agreed under cross-examination (Day 95, para 19B) that there will be 286,000 m^3 by the year 2081, even if not a single station is built after Torness and Heysham II (stations now under construction). This figure excludes all wastes from Ministry of Defence operations, and those from foreign contracts. The extended period allows for continuing operations for decommissioning. This total is an inescapable commitment. The agreed CEGB and BNFL estimate (in Document C1/44 Res) for intermediate-level wastes from the whole life of Sizewell B, including decommissioning, is 4,000 m^3. In view of this, the suggestion that 'the creation of wastes from nuclear activity might be minimised by building no more nuclear power-stations than are absolutely necessary', made by Mr Blake during his cross-examination, seems eminently sensible (Day 95, para 23C).

56. *WP Paragraphs 36 and 53.* Concerning the disposal of intermediate level wastes, for thirty years these have been allowed to accumulate without apparently a thought being given to any means of tackling them. This was the object

of severe reproof by the Royal Commission. Mr Wedd (Day 100, para 35B) mentions the 'inconvenience and expense' of looking after intermediate level wastes, and in his own evidence (DoE/P/1, para 6.4) says: 'There is no technical advantage to be gained in delaying disposal of these wastes; furthermore, the availability of suitable disposal facilities will save the construction of additional stores . . . the government's stated intention of giving priority to making progress towards the early disposal of these wastes has been generally welcomed.' A splendid exercise in making a virtue of necessity, and in transforming criticism into general approval. Meanwhile we have paid for thirty years' storage.

57. There is now a quarter of a ton of plutonium in the Irish Sea. It would be beyond belief had it not happened, that it could ever have been thought permissible to throw out this stuff into the living environment without any proper scientific examination of the results of such action. Even if the totally unjustified assumption that it would remain conveniently stuck in the sediments on the sea bed had been correct, had they never heard of the habit of plaice and other flatfish of lying precisely there?

58. The question of the plutonium being washed up onto the shore, dried out and then blown onto the land, was raised at the Windscale Enquiry. The inspector had air tests carried out which (it was pointed out at the time by the objectors) were inadequate for any proper scientific appraisal; but he swept these arguments aside. It was also pointed out that, without being airborne, the plutonium could be carried into houses in the mud on fishermen's boots.

59. It has happened exactly as the objectors said, and this has been shown up, not by the 'regulatory bodies', but by a band of heroic amateurs, who were promptly fined £50,000 for their efforts to protect us. There has been either a total failure to monitor the place properly, or else eyes have been deliberately closed so that costs of waste

treatment should not become embarrassing to the industry. There has been cynical neglect of the public interest.

60. In the last sentence of para 36, surely 'a modified mine or purpose-built cavity' would be open to the same objections and dangers as were described at the borehole Enquiry?

61. *WP Paragraphs 43 and 44.* These mention SIXEP, an ion-exchange plant to obviate as far as possible the discharge of caesium 137 from the Magnox cooling ponds to the Irish Sea. How much does this cost? Anyway the damage has been done. Caesium 137 is dangerously radioactive for over 500 years, and is water-soluble, thus passing up the food-chain through a vast number of organisms in its lifetime. It is sheer madness to poison our life-support systems like this. Did the people responsible never have the simple thought that perhaps it might be better to close down the Magnox stations until the problem was solved, instead of leaking caesium 137 for nearly thirty years as they have done, before attempting to stop it? Not at all. Nuclear power is the crown of human achievement and sacrosanct.

62. *WP Paragraph 57.* 'The Royal Commission recommended that a Nuclear Waste Disposal Corporation should be set up as an independent statutory body to develop and manage disposal facilities . . . instead, the government has agreed that the component parts of the industry should, in co-operation, set up a Nuclear Industry Radioactive Waste Executive (NIREX) . . .'

63. Responsibility for radioactive waste management was taken from the nuclear industry and passed to DoE so that the public could have confidence that it was under the control of a totally impartial body. But in the light of the above quote, the suggestion that handing the responsibility for waste-management policies to DoE would make it 'independent of the responsibilities for promoting nuclear power' sounds very hollow. Yet it was this independence, above all, that the Royal Commission sought. Instead,

NIREX, consisting entirely of 'component parts of the industry' and based at Harwell, neither meets this desideratum nor inspires confidence.

63. On top of this, Mr Hookway says in his evidence (DoE/P/2, para 7.16): 'Potential land-disposal facilities for intermediate level wastes will be dealt with by NIREX in their evidence in support of CEGB.' WHY should NIREX support CEGB? Their job is to get rid of the wastes, not to promote the creation of more. This is just a first sample of the results of handing back the executive part of waste management to the sole control of the industry itself; it strengthens the suspicion of the public, that the first concern of the nuclear industry is its own perpetuation.

65. It also has an inbuilt tendency to dictatorship, of which there was an unpleasant instance last summer. Sir Peter Hirsch, Chairman of UKAEA, said on Channel 4 early in June that local authorities must eventually agree to underground sites being used for the disposal of intermediate radioactive nuclear waste. He suspected that 'there are ways of doing this by offering them something.' At this the Ordinary Citizen's blood really does boil. Note the 'must', and the pressure to be applied. By what right does Sir Peter Hirsch dictate to local councils elected by their people? We have heard about freedom and democracy *ad nauseam* during the last year or two, we don't need to be told, they are the British birthright, but it seems we shall have to start defending them in our own backyard.

66. Another area in which the Royal Commission wanted more independence from the industry was in RWMAC: 'The Advisory Committee should have a strong environmental representation (R.C. Report, para 428).' There is none at all in the official sense, only one individual – nobody from the Council for the Preservation of Rural England (CPRE), Friends of the Earth (FOE), the Nature Conservancy Council (NCC), Countryside Commission, Civic Trust, or any other such body. There is no local authority representation either. Why not? There should

surely be two or three drawn preferably from the counties
where there are nuclear installations, and including one at
least from the Windscale area. There should also be at
least one member of the public from the local liaison
committees of these installations.

67. *WP Paragraph 58.* . . . 'The regulatory bodies . . . will
ensure . . . that the public are fully safeguarded, both now
and for future generations.' Really? A statement which
has no basis in law, as no government in this country can
bind a succeeding one.

68. *WP Paragraph 62.* The public now has very little
faith in public enquiries (which are also mentioned in
paragraphs 35, 37 and 68), especially since the previous
energy minister declared his intention of going ahead with
the Sizewell B PWR station whatever the result of the
enquiry.

69. 'Involving the Public'. Turning to the final section of
the White Paper, the only possible comment on it is that,
if the proposed reports are like this one, their only effect
will be to 'exaggerate' public concern still further. Paragraph 12 says: 'The main task is to identify the most
appropriate of the methods available to us for each category of waste and then ensure that this method is im-
plemented . . .' It is now nearly thirty years since Calder
Hall was built, and the weapons reactor was working at
Windscale and producing wastes for some years before
that. It is absolutely staggering that the people involved in
dealing with the entirely new and uniquely dangerous
elements emerging in these wastes didn't get the whole of
this treatment-disposal question settled before they went
on with the programme, and bring it all to a halt if they
couldn't solve it. They hardly even tried. The irresponsibility was criminal.

70. Those who followed have been no better. The statement in para 22 that the 'Environment Departments have
set in hand . . . the preparation of an overall long-term
strategy for the management of wastes' is a glaring ex-

posure of the attitude that has prevailed for all these
years. The Royal Commission found it 'surprising'. A more
drastic adjective would have been appropriate.

71. Subparagraph 13(v) highlights the same situation. DoE
has the responsibility to 'ensure that there is adequate
research and development on methods of disposal'. The
Royal Commission also said (paragraph 337 – after their
statement of principle): 'We are clear that such a demonstration will require a substantial programme of research.'
If all this massive research is still needed, why does this
White Paper say, as quoted in WP Paragraph 66, that the
problems can all be solved by 'the systematic application
of known technology'?

72. UKAEA has had hundreds of millions in grants from
the government, which should have insisted that the wastes
question had absolute priority, in view of previous neglect.
UKAEA, on the contrary, has always devoted by far the
largest slice of the funds provided to the development of
the fast breeder. They have blithely assumed all along that
vitrification of HLW and putting them in deep holes in the
ground would settle all that – no worry – but did nothing
to prove beyond all reasonable doubt that this would
work. But when the borehole question is subjected to 'the
application of sound common sense', deep irretrievable
disposal is found, quite rightly, to be unacceptable.

73. How can the government ask for 'public support based
on a full and accurate assessment of the situation' when,
in such a dangerous technology as this, the Nuclear Installations Inspectorate (NII) and the monitoring section of
the Ministry of Agriculture, Fisheries and Food (MAFF)
are understaffed and underpaid and are obviously unable
to keep up with their appointed tasks? The fact that billions
are lavished on the industry, while the watchdog organisations are starved of resources, when the protection of the
public should be the absolute priority, reduces all the
smooth assurances of the White Paper to the status of mere
bureaucratic waffle.

74. The relevant proceedings at the Sizewell B enquiry only increase this impression, as already explained. They also add an element of sheer bewilderment.

75. The public has been promised all along that a PWR would not be built in this country until a full enquiry had been held into the problem of its safety. Need and cost are other important aspects, but it is obviously futile to dismiss these unless the safety question has been satisfactorily settled, and has been seen to be settled in full and open public discussion.

76. When the NII's Report on this, the essential basis for the argument, was found not to be ready after the enquiry had been opened, and was seen to be receding further and further into the future, objectors naturally asked for an adjournment. It was pointed out that six months were needed for effective study of the report. After five months this request was refused, during which time the enquiry acquired momentum and its own kind of vested interest. It was then discovered that the NII report would not merely be late, but that it would not be completed until the enquiry was all over; moreover that eighty major flaws in the PWR design had been identified. How could this situation not have been known by the government, and why was the enquiry not delayed until the most important evidence to be put before it was complete? The government's promises are cynically broken, and the enquiry reduced to a farce. The NII has so few resources that it can't do its proper work, while CEGB spends millions and has taken six years to prepare its case.

77. CEGB has admitted in its evidence (Day 95, para 66G), that the Sizewell B station 'will not be needed until 1997 on grounds of electricity demand'. The Ordinary Citizen had thought innocently that demand was the usual reason for building power stations. In other words, a breathing space of five years is available.

78. There is another reason for delaying Sizewell B. CEGB itself piously quotes in its own evidence (CEGB/S/8, para

21) the lines laid down by the Royal Commission: 'The Commission recommended that there should be no commitment to a large-scale nuclear programme until it has been demonstrated beyond reasonable doubt . . .' (not DoE's beloved 'established in principle', note) '. . . that a method exists to ensure the safe containment of long-lived, highly radioactive waste for the indefinite future . . . *the Commission's proposition is bound to be the dominant factor in any process preceding decisions about further large-scale programmes . . .*'. And note that it does not say '*a* dominant factor' but '*the* dominant factor', which in any normal interpretation would mean that it is paramount.

79. That CEGB is fully aware of the state of the art in the waste management field is shown by the following evidence. Day 95, para 11B–C quotes para 22 of CEGB/ S/142: 'The Environment Departments have set in hand, in consultation with the nuclear industry, the generating boards and other organisations, the preparation of an overall long-term strategy for management of wastes, including those at present stored at nuclear sites.' This is followed by a statement by Mr Wedd (para 11D) that this strategy '. . . is in the course of preparation and revision and is likely to remain in that state for a long time to come'.

80. So much for the theoretical side: what is the state of affairs in brute fact on the ground? Briefly:

(a) There are uncertainties about THORP.

(b) The vitrification plant is only on the drawing-board, though the building to contain it is up.

(c) The engineered store to hold the vitrified blocks for fifty years (or in perpetuity?) is not even on the drawing-board or quoted for, or the site settled, despite the fact that, if AVM comes into operation by 1989 as promised, the store must be ready and in full running order to receive the glass blocks by then.

(d) Getting beyond 'established in principle' for deep disposal on land has been put off for fifty years (with

obvious relief – it will be someone else's pigeon by
then), and there are very serious question marks over
it anyway.

(e) Deep sea disposal is not even 'established in principle'.

81. Such being the situation on the waste-disposal front, if
the Royal Commission's proposition 'is bound to be the
dominant factor in any process preceding decisions about
further large-scale programmes', why is this enquiry sitting
at all? CEGB has spent £6 million preparing its case, and
the immense cost of the enquiry (borne entirely by CEGB)
will all end up in our electricity bills. The mental processes
at work here are simply not normal or consistent or indeed
rational. For CEGB to quote this passage, yet not use the
five-year leeway which it admits it has in order to make
some attempt to meet the Royal Commission's standard,
is grossly cynical.

82. Moreover, RWMAC's fourth report (para 6.2) points
out that:

. . . the governments of a number of countries, such
as Denmark, the FRG, the Netherlands, Sweden and
Switzerland, have made developments or further development of nuclear power conditional on acceptable schemes for disposing of high-level wastes. Ultimately, the
implementation of such schemes will depend on the
scientific and technical demonstration of their feasibility
and cost-effectiveness, and on the degree of public confidence they can command.

This is the same as our Royal Commission's principle, but
definitely adopted instead of being given mere lip service.
The present experience has proved that the inclusion of
such principles in the publications of the bodies involved
in this country is nothing but empty ritual, which has
destroyed the ordinary citizen's faith in any such statements
from now on.

83. *WP Annex*. My final comment concerns Section (a) of the Annex which reads: 'All practices . . .' (yes, *all*) '. . . giving rise to radioactive wastes must be justified, i.e. the need for the practice must be established in terms of its overall benefit'.

84. If the government *means* this (which of course it doesn't – we get floods of propaganda but no cool judgment), it should suspend the Sizewell B enquiry and set up a Royal Commission to look into every aspect of the nuclear industry. This should include a drastic examination of its whole record (UKAEA, BNFL, CEGB, South of Scotland Electricity Board, MAFF), with a dispassionate look at what the public has got for its money, which runs into many billions, some of them concealed under other headings; money which has been taken from, not voted by, the public. Why are these billions never, never cut, while everything else is? Some of the numerous financial aspects requiring investigation are listed in the Appendix.

Conclusion

85. To sum up, Cmnd 8607 is a very depressing document. The frequent expressions in it of the government's 'beliefs', 'convictions', and 'considered judgments' are contradicted by the facts which are glaring.

86. Such a policy shows that the government has learnt nothing from the mistakes of the pioneers; on the contrary, it is repeating them, brazenly, on a larger scale, and of set purpose. Royal Commission principles, its own DoE, White Papers and regulations resulting from them, any idea that radioactive wastes present any problem at all, are ruthlessly swept aside. It is left to DoE to put what decent-seeming façade it can on the situation, a job that would tax a super-Machiavelli: hence, no doubt, the strange discrepancies that have been quoted.

87. However, DoE's Report No. 32 of 1979 says honestly

and openly (para 4.3.3): 'The isolation of disposed waste from the environment cannot, of course, be guaranteed in perpetuity.' So the Royal Commission's requirements cannot be met, and the nuclear power industry as such is therefore 'irresponsible and morally wrong'. But the priority from the start until now has always been to preserve it at all costs (immense ones), any other consideration being secondary.

88. The inescapable burden now inflicted on posterity imposes a straight moral choice, which was not faced in the beginning but which must be faced now. Even a desperate need for energy would not justify creating these worst of all pollutants, whose control for merely a few centuries (in the case of HLW) we cannot guarantee, far less that of the long-lived actinides which are forever. We have not even a moderate need for this technology, never mind a desperate one.

89. This is a failed and dying industry, which is a major liability and should be closed down. The fact that plans can be made for adding to it shows an unbelievable degree of irresponsibility and stupidity in all concerned.

90. The Ordinary Citizen implores the inspector to urge the right moral choice on the government, which should redirect all its spare billions towards energy conservation, cleaning up fossil-fuelled power stations, and developing alternative energy sources.

Appendix

Financial aspects of the nuclear industry requiring investigation include the following:

1. Capital Costs. The capital costs of Windscale, Springfields, Risley, Capenhurst, Harwell and Winfrith. The nuclear industry was presented with these by the Ministry of Works which had held them for Defence – and all

running and ready staffed. Has a reasonable proportion of the cost ever been debited to the industry?

2. Research and development (R and D). The basic R and D had likewise all been done by UKAEA for years and even now is only charged as to 50 per cent. It must have been, and still be, some of the most intricate, extensive and expensive R and D ever done.

(What other industry has ever had these two enormous starting costs handed to it on a plate? Both (1) and (2) were probably lost in the defence budget. There should be no taking refuge in the Official Secrets Act over this: what happened twenty-five to thirty years ago can't interest anybody except the ordinary citizen who provided the cash.)

3. Grants. Total of grants to UKAEA since it was set up (£200,000,000 last year). These grants go through Parliament 'on the nod', and appear never to be questioned or criticised. They come from the Department of Energy's fund for scientific and industrial R and D, of which the AEA got nearly threequarters in 1981–82 (total of the fund £216 million, AEA grant £172 million). Out of the remainder, £1 million was spent on solar energy and £500,000 on energy conservation! The largest proportion by far of their annual grant goes on running the Dounreay establishment and into research into the FBR generally. They also do research on the programme of thermal reactors as follows:

(a) The essential research for the Magnox programme was done before general commercial building started, as noted under 2 above. How much has been spent on Magnox research since, which has not been charged to the industry?

(b) Only in 1967 did CEGB start paying a very small royalty to AEA. By that time all the basic research for the AGR programme was done. Has the cost of this research been added to the capital cost of AGR?

(For continuing AGR research, see under 'Nuclear Energy Vote' below.)

(c) CEGB now pay for 50 per cent (only) of the research done for it by AEA. When did it start to do this? A recoupment of 50 per cent on AGR R and D is mentioned in paragraph 8 of AEA's 1981–82 report. Is the other 50 per cent counted as part of the cost of the AGR programme?

(d) The same applies to PWR. At the Sizewell B enquiry, on Day 47, when asked whether 'in the context of an investment appraisal, one is looking to the future, rather than the past in the context of research costs which may have been spent in the past which are attributable to the project under review', Mr Priddle replied: 'Yes, that is exactly right. Costs in the past are *sunk costs* and are therefore *not relevant*.' Brazil should try this one! So not only is the 50 per cent of the cost of research for the Sizewell programme lost in the AEA grant, but the other 50 per cent which the CEGB *does* bear, is sunk without trace (under the ocean-bed?), and considered 'not relevant'. Only future research on Sizewell B will be taken into account. Just where does CEGB put this 50 per cent in their accounts? If in some general fund, it will be spread over the whole generating field, thus unfairly altering the balance between the costs of the conventional and nuclear sections. In any case the PWR programme is made out to be cheaper than it really is. What is the total sum so far spent on PWR R and D?

(e) What is the total so far spent on the FBR, to include research by the AEA, and the total spent on construction and running at Dounreay?

4. Magnox cost. Total capital cost of the Magnox programme, including a fair estimate for R and D (see above). CEGB's admission recently that coal-fired stations would have been cheaper is probably only the tip of the iceberg.

And what are the total interest charges since inception? A proportion of the cost equal to the downrating of all these stations was written off – but it *was* a cost, and was paid for somehow. How?

5. AGR cost. Total capital cost of the AGR programme to the end of 1982, including interest charges (a major financial disaster, this one). Was the downrating proportion written off, as for Magnox?

(Both programmes being a dead loss, is it reasonable to expect any ordinary citizen to believe that the next one (PWR) will be any better? The whole civil nuclear programme to date has been a gigantic financial failure, which would have been abandoned long ago in any free play of market forces. Only vast government subvention has kept it going, both here and in America.

It now appears that the interest charges on these enormous capital costs were paid out of CEGB revenue, thus making the price of electricity to the consumer considerably higher than it need have been. Why has Parliament never demanded a full public exposure of the whole fiasco? Presumably the interest on the Magnox capital borrowing was paid in the same way. Have these charges been debited to the nuclear section, or have they been spread over the whole CEGB operations, resulting in distortion of comparisons between the fossil and nuclear sections?)

6. Nuclear Energy Vote. There was at the beginning of this decade, and probably still is, a fund called the Nuclear Energy Vote. At that time it was being used for research into improvements to the AGRs under construction. Have the sums spent in this way been counted in the cost of AGRs? How long has this fund been running, how much money has it absorbed during the whole of its existence, how is it funded, and who, if anybody, controls it?

7. Magnox waste costs. Extension and 'refurbishing' of Magnox cooling ponds and reprocessing plant at Windscale have absorbed *several hundred million pounds* within the last five years. DoE's report No. 32 says that 'existing and

planned storage capacity for Magnox fuel cladding (solid HLW) will be full by 1985'. What will more of this cost?

8. The Nuclear Installations Inspectorate costs. There can be very little of its work that is not concerned with some part of the production of nuclear electricity and the disposal of its wastes, and the industry should be charged accordingly. This item is probably lost in the accounts of the Health and Safety Executive, in which they were merged a few years ago, to their own great resentment.

9. Police cost. The total cost of the armed police (600 or more strong) guarding nuclear installations. Presumably the armed forces guard what concerns them. This police force is almost certainly paid for by the Secret Service, to which technically it belongs, and the real cost of nuclear power is thus reduced.

10. Other waste treatment costs. Total cost of waste treatment up to 1971 when BNFL was set up. These costs are totally repudiated by BNFL, but were mentioned every year in their report for years, with the comment that they were substantial. They were then completely ignored by everybody. In 1983 the government at last agreed to take over such parts of these costs as referred to their own departments, which presumably means the defence contribution to these wastes. That leaves all the waste treatment resulting from the Magnox programme up to 1971. How much does this amount to, and under what heading will the ordinary citizen be called upon to pay it? What interest charges have accumulated since 1971? All this should be added to the cost of Magnox.

11. BNFL grants. Total of grants to BNFL since it was set up in 1971.

12. Outage costs. Total cost of all outages and breakdowns in all nuclear power stations to date. There is more than a suspicion that when coal-fired stations are brought in to fill these gaps in supply, the costs of running them are charged against the coal-fired section of the industry, thus of course making coal-produced electricity appear that

much dearer. The cost of replacement of current is caused by the nuclear section and should be charged against it.

13. Reprocessing contracts. Full details of the reprocessing contract with Japan concerning THORP, and of contracts with European countries for reprocessing. If BNFL is making such large profits as are rumoured out of these operations, it only shows what enormous sums other countries will pay to get rid of these embarrassing by-products, and how utterly foolish we are to make our own nuclear industry possible by fouling our small nest with this dreadful stuff.

14. THORP costs. Probable capital cost of THORP by completion date, plus interest, and how funded. Running costs. Successor costs?

15. Vitrification costs. Probable capital cost of the vitrification plant, plus interest, and how funded. Running costs. By 1980, £3½ million had already been written off development costs. Total cost of HARVEST (all wasted).

16. Vitrification store costs. Capital cost of engineered store to take vitrified HLW for fifty years (or longer?), and running costs.

17. HLW tanks cost. Present cost of stainless steel tanks for liquid HLW.

18. Flask costs. Six of the massive steel 'flasks' in which the spent fuel is transported to Windscale are now to be replaced because of possible defects, at a cost of £350,000 each (£2,100,000 total). How many of these flasks are there altogether, and how often do they have to be replaced? (fifty tons of steel to carry two tons of waste!). This is only for the journey to where all the vastly expensive treatment begins; yet CEGB at the enquiry so far lost its sense of proportion as to think it necessary to mention the cost of the removal of fly-ash from coal-fired stations when drawing a comparison!

19. Waste-dumping ship cost. Capital cost and running costs.

20. Monitoring cost. No proper estimate can be made at

all of the cost of cooling and monitoring HLW for 500 to 600 years, nor of the same for even longer-lived actinides; nor of the loss of health, food sources and amenity. By the end of the day – if there still is one – they must vastly exceed all items 1 to 19 together.

21. Endowment fund. Cost of a massive endowment fund to be provided for posterity, as some sort of acknowledgement of, and compensation for, this thing which we are inflicting on them. It can't really compensate, but it is a minimum decency.

MINUTES OF EVIDENCE TAKEN BEFORE THE HOME AFFAIRS
COMMITTEE

30 January 1985

Rt Hon L. Brittan, QC, MP, Mr M. J. A. Partridge, CB,
Mr P. R. A. Fulton and Sir L. Byford, CBE, QPM

On Wednesday January 30th, 1984 the Home Secretary,
the Rt Hon. Leon Brittan, appeared before the House of
Commons Home Affairs Committee which is looking into
the activities and responsibilities of the Special Branch,
that special police force formed in 1883 to track down Irish
terrorists who had been placing bombs in buildings. At
that stage it was known as the Special Irish Branch. After
three years 'Irish' was dropped from the Branch's title and
it was expanded to deal with security issues in general.

Present at the Home Affairs Committee that day, chaired by Sir Edward Gardner, were Gerald Bermingham,
Robin Corbett, Janet Fookes, Jeremy Hanley, John Hunt,
Clare Short, Ivor Stanbrook, John Wheeler and David
Winnick. The home secretary had already expressed himself as 'lukewarm' over the Committee investigating this
particular subject.

During the session he was questioned on to whom the Special Branch were accountable and on how he defined subversion, to which he gave the following answers:

Mr Wheeler

489. Could I clear up one point on Mr Hanley's questions? Home Secretary, my friend and colleague, Mr Hanley, used a phrase, in respect of the Special Branch, in which he suggested it was accountable to the security services. I am sure you would wish to clear up that point?

(Mr *Brittan*.) Certainly. I did not want to pick up Mr Hanley on that, but it is not the case that they are accountable to the security service. They do work under the aegis of the security service, but they are, of course, accountable only to the chief constable. They are under the chief constable of their force. In the last analysis, if the security service were to request him to do that which he did not think appropriate (which, I hasten to add, is *not* something which occurs), it would be for the chief constable to decide whether the Special Branch should or should not comply with the request.

Mr Corbett

490. Home Secretary, you issued a copy of your reply to John Prescott as a news release. Did you consider issuing it to this Committee, and reject it, or did it not cross your mind?

(Mr *Brittan*.) I thought that this Committee would ask questions of a more substantial and detailed kind than is reflected in the comparatively brief answer that I gave to Mr Prescott, and I did not think that this Committee would be complimented by treating the answer (which was an answer to a written request in a letter written in a perfectly normal way) as being an aspect of my evidence.

491. If it was so lightweight, why then was it issued as a press release?

(Mr *Brittan*.) Because it was a matter to which Mr Prescott, I think you will find, attached considerable importance, and it seemed to me right that I should reply and give those who were interested in it an opportunity to see what I had to say.

492. I hear what you say. However, you have, twice this afternoon and earlier in the House of Commons on December 10th, made this quite clear. This is column 737 in Hansard, when you were asked by the Member for Manchester, Gorton, about an allegation of telephone tapping and interference with the mail of the CND. You say here: 'There is no doubt that peaceful political campaigning to change the mind of the government and of people generally about the validity of nuclear disarmament, whether unilateral or otherwise, is an entirely legitimate activity.' You repeated the same sentiment column 740. In paragraph 16 of the guidelines which were so surprisingly published as an unexpected Christmas present, it says: 'Data on individuals or organisations should not under any circumstances be collected or held solely on the basis that such a person or organisation supports unpopular causes.' That is still your view, is it, Home Secretary?

(Mr *Brittan*.) Oh yes, I have not changed my view since December. Can I just, though, answer that on a very small point? It has been drawn to my attention (since we are looking at Hansard) that I gave the wrong dates for my statements. One was indeed January 22nd, the other was October 22nd and not December 22nd which I may have given. For the record, let us get that right.

493. But against that background, Home Secretary, how can you then, in your letter to Mr Prescott (a copy of which I have obtained), say in paragraph 5: 'The definition' (that is, of Lord Harris) 'is not limited to possible acts of a

criminal nature.' – and this is the bit I would like your comment on – 'In an open society such as ours, it is all too easy to use tactics which are not themselves unlawful for subversive ends, and those who are entrusted with safeguarding our democratic institutions from subversive attack must not be prevented from looking into the activities of those whose real aim is to harm our democracy, but who for tactical or other reasons choose to keep either in the long or the short term within the letter of the law in what they do.'? How do you square *that* statement with the earlier statements which you made? With respect, they just seem to be in violent collision.

(Mr *Brittan*.) They are certainly not in violent collision. There is nothing that requires squaring. There is nothing in the least inconsistent between the one and the other. I was simply saying, perfectly simply, that people are entitled to have political views, they are entitled to campaign in favour of them, and that is not in any way subversive. However, the combination of the two limbs of Lord Harris's definition defines what is subversion. When you have activities which both threaten the safety and well-being of the State *and* which are intended to undermine or overthrow parliamentary democracy, that *is* subversion. What one is saying is that it is not in the least surprising that there should be people who are not engaged in criminal activities at that stage, but who do have as their aim the overthrow or the undermining of parliamentary democracy, and who *are* engaged in activities that threaten the safety or well-being of the State. I see nothing inconsistent in it at all.

494. Let me try to put it another way, Home Secretary. It must be so in logic, must it not, that one interpretation put on that part of this letter is that every single man and woman in this country is a potential subversive, under what you have written in this letter?

(Mr *Brittan*.) I do not think that for one single moment, and nor does anyone else.

495. But in logic, any of us might be capable, in some circumstances, well into the future, of behaving in a way, even under the guidelines definition of 'Subversion' which could be interpreted by a Special Branch officer in any one of forty-three police forces (no national police force), as being a potential subversive. It must follow, must it not?

(Mr *Brittan*.) What you have said just now is absolutely nothing to do with the definition of 'subversion'. For activities to count as subversive, it is not sufficient that you might engage in something at some time. Activities, to be subversive, have actually to threaten the safety or well-being of the State *and* to be intended to undermine or overthrow parliamentary democracy. It seems to me that unless you focus on both limbs of that definition, you are doing less than justice to the guidelines in which that definition is now embodied. It just is not the case to say that everybody in the country could be regarded as subversive, by applying those guidelines. If we are talking about logic, I am afraid I would have to disagree with you as to where the logic leads.

496. Let us see where we get with the meaning of words. You say here: 'for tactical or other reasons choose to keep either in the long or the short term within the letter of the law in what they do.' The assumption behind this is that they are so smart and they are so 'boned up' on the law (although, incidentally, there is no test of lawfulness in the definition of 'subversion', but we will leave that on one side), that they behave lawfully at this point, but somebody somewhere says, 'But they don't mean it', they make that judgment. It is in *that* sense that I say that when that subjective judgment is made, each and every one of us is capable of becoming a potential subversive. It must follow, must it not?

(Mr *Brittan*.) But it does not follow for one second, because you have studiously refused to look at the other limb of the argument of definition. You are, it seems to me, *not* pursuing a logical course, in refusing to do that. I have repeatedly said that for there to be subversion, the activities have to threaten the safety or well-being of the State, not something which might happen some time in the future. Indeed, at that point, it is activities which threaten the safety or well-being of the State, not which somebody might think could at some time do that. So that is one limb of the argument. The other is 'which are intended to undermine or overthrow Parliamentary democracy'. Indeed, the subjective element is the intention, but it is not unusual in our society for there to be a requirement that somebody has to assess what somebody else's intention is. That is what is happening all the time. You seem to be suggesting that there was some problem about the fact of whether something was lawful or unlawful. There is no mystery about it at all. It is perfectly clear that subversion, under this definition, includes activity which is not a criminal offence. If that were *not* required, if that were not so, there would not be any need for a definition of this kind. But I beg you to believe that if you confined your activities as a Special Branch to where there has actually been a breach of the criminal law, you would certainly be failing to obtain information about a large number of activities which every single person in this room would regard as subversive.

497. I am still puzzled, Home Secretary. You have helped on one point, and I am grateful to you, but you are saying that there are some activities which, although not criminal in themselves, may meet the one leg of that definition of 'subversion'. Can you give an example of this? [The Home Secretary refused to give any such examples.]